What's
the
Difference?

By the Same Author

CHRISTIAN PRIMER

What's the Difference?

A COMPARISON OF THE FAITHS MEN LIVE BY

LOUIS CASSELS

1965

Doubleday & Company, Inc., Garden City, New York

Library of Congress Catalog Card Number 65-17248
Copyright © 1965 by Louis Cassels
All Rights Reserved
Printed in the United States of America

To my son, Michael,
who sets me a good example of respect for
the beliefs of others, this book is
affectionately dedicated

Contents

A Preliminary Word to the Reader 1

I THE VARIETIES OF FAITH 5

The Beliefs of the Atheists; Hedonism: Faith in Pleasure; Humanism: Faith in Man; Communism: Faith in Materialism; The Varieties of Pantheism; Primitive Animism; Classic and Modern Polytheism; Spinoza, Emerson, and the Bishop of Woolwich; The Faith in One God; The Personal God

II THE JEWISH-CHRISTIAN
   HERITAGE 21

The Vision of Abraham; Moses and the Chosen People; Jesus of Nazareth; Did the Jews Reject Jesus?; The Dazzling Light of the Resurrection; Jewish and Christian Concepts; Changing Attitudes; Must Man Save Himself?; Evan-

gelism and Conversion; Orthodox, Conservative, and Reform Judaism; Who Is a Jew?

III THE CATHOLIC-PROTESTANT
DIFFERENCES   41

Grace and Faith—Different Meanings; The Authority of the Bishops; "Upon This Rock . . ."; Can the Church Err?; The Authority of Scripture; Who Interprets Scripture?; The Adoration of Mary; A New Catholic Viewpoint; Saints, Purgatory, and Merit; Two Sacraments or Seven?; Baptism; The Lord's Supper; The Changing Forms of Worship

IV IS THE BIBLE INFALLIBLE?   63

When Luther and Calvin Disagreed; The Birth of Liberalism; The Social Gospel; Fundamentalism; Salvation and Piety; Modern Orthodoxy; The Radical Reinterpreters; The Evangelicals

V THE PROTESTANT FAITH
FAMILIES: THE GREAT
REFORMATION CHURCHES   79

THE LUTHERANS; *Indulgences for Sale; A Spark in Dry Tinder; The Lutherans Today; Lutheran Worship;*

THE PRESBYTERIANS; *What Calvin Taught; Lutheran-Calvinist Differences; The Origin of "Presbyterian"; The American Presbyterians; The Order of Worship*; THE ANGLICANS; *The Book of Common Prayer; Are Anglicans Protestant or Catholic?; Episcopalians— the American Anglicans; The Episcopal Appeal*

VI THE PURITAN HERITAGE
THE CONGREGATIONALISTS;   109

The Pilgrims; The Congregational Stamp on American Life; The United Church of Christ; THE BAPTISTS; *The Anabaptists; America's Debt to Roger Williams; The Baptist Groups Today; How Baptists Worship*

VII MORE MOVEMENTS BORN OF
THE CHURCH OF ENGLAND   123

THE METHODISTS; *The Aldersgate Experience; The Circuit Riders; The Efficient Organizers; Prohibition and Abstinence; "Think and Let Think"; A Middle-class Denomination*; SOCIETY OF FRIENDS; *George Fox's Inner Light; The Persecuted Friends; Turning the Other Cheek*; THE MENNONITES; *The Amish and the Hutterian Brethren*

VIII   THE FAITHS BORN IN
AMERICA   143

THE CHRISTIANS; *The Patriarchs of
the Movement; No Creed but Christ;
The Rift in the Movement;* UNITARI-
ANS AND UNIVERSALISTS; *The
New England Unitarianism; The Evolu-
tion of Universalism; Preoccupation
with Social Problems;* THE MOR-
MONS; *The Persecuted; The Polygamy
Issue; Distinctive Mormon Doctrines;*
SEVENTH-DAY ADVENTISTS; *The
Most Generous Fundamentalists; The
Second Advent and Emphasis on
Health;* CHRISTIAN SCIENTISTS;
Their Basic Philosophy; THE PENTE-
COSTALS; *The Gift of Tongues;* THE
HOLINESS CHURCHES; JEHO-
VAH'S WITNESSES; *Expectance of
Armageddon; Heaven for the Few Only*

IX   THE EASTERN ORTHODOX   175

*The Great Schism; Orthodox and
Catholic Similarities; The Orthodox in
America*

X   ISLAM AND THE MOSLEMS   183

*The Prophet of Allah; The Koran;
"The Five Pillars of Islam"; The Pil-
grimage to Mecca; The Moral Rules;
The Expansion of Islam*

XI THE ORIENTAL RELIGIONS   195

HINDUISM; *The Concept of Reincarnation; The Caste System;* BUDDHISM; *The "Four Noble Truths"; Two Distinct Kinds of Buddhism; The Real Zen*

XII DOES IT MATTER WHAT YOU
     BELIEVE?   211

Modern Syncretism; Why Christians Can't Compromise

Other Books to Read   219

What's the Difference?

A Preliminary Word to the Reader

During the years I have functioned as religion editor of United Press International, I've been asked a great many questions by newspaper readers (and, I might add, by newspaper editors, who are every bit as curious as they are popularly supposed to be, although perhaps not quite as omniscient). Some of the questions are evidently rhetorical. To this category I assign such inquiries as "How can you write such tripe?" and "Where on earth did you get the ridiculous notion that . . . ?"

Of those that are seriously intended to elicit information, a very large percentage seem to begin with the words "What's the difference . . . ?" I have concluded that there are quite a number of people around—intelligent, well-disposed, fair-minded people—who want to know how their religious beliefs differ from those of their neighbors.

It is for them, primarily, that this book was written. But I will confess that I also cherish the hope that it may prove helpful to an altogether different type of reader—the person who hasn't any well-thought-out convictions of his own and who is looking around to see what religious options are available to modern man.

The opening chapters deal with basic differences that mark off broad areas of religious spectrum. In Chapter I we will consider how theistic religion (a category that includes Christianity, Judaism, and Islam) differs from pantheism and atheism.

In Chapter II, we will focus on the two theistic religions that are of principal importance in America—Christianity and Judaism.

Chapter III takes up differences between Catholics and Protestants. And Chapter IV examines the main camps into which Protestants are divided.

The remaining chapters are devoted to a study of the distinctive aspects of various Protestant denominations, and other religious faiths which have not been covered previously. The reader who plugs away to the bitter end will acquire at least a smattering of information—I would hope more than a smattering—about most of the religions, from animism to Zen, that command the allegiance of significant numbers of human beings in the world today.

I am sure that I shall live to rue that last sentence. I can see the letters now: "How could you overlook Neo-Zoroastrianism? We have five people here in Fickle Falls who meet every Tuesday night to discuss this new faith, and we are thinking of building a church. . . ."

So let me apologize in advance to any reader who feels that his particular religious viewpoint has been overlooked, or given short shrift. Without writing an encyclopedia, it would not be possible to deal separately and adequately with each of the 275 religious bodies listed in the *Yearbook of American Churches.* In the space available, I've tried to concentrate on the religious differences that seem to be most basic, or which affect fairly large numbers of people.

Let me give fair warning, however: This is *not* an "objective" book, if by objective you understand that the author is neutral, impartial, or indifferent. I do not see how it is possible for anyone to be truly neutral about religion; some of the most viciously slanted books I've ever read were written by people who make a great noise about their "objectivity."

So I think you are entitled to know that I write as a committed Christian, who has been nourished in the Protestant tradition. I look at other religions, inevitably, through Protestant Christian eyes, and I am sure that this orientation will be quite obvious to the discerning reader.

However, I have also been trained, during more than twenty years as a wire-service reporter, to be as fair and accurate as humanly possible in presenting the other fellow's point of view. Even if UPI had not pounded this maxim into my head, I hope that my own conscience would not permit me to malign or knowingly misrepresent any person's religious faith. If anyone feels that I have been unjust to his beliefs in this book, I do not merely apologize: I humbly beg his forgiveness.

L.C.

CHAPTER I

The Varieties of Faith

Everyone has a religion of some kind.

There are people who call themselves unbelievers or insist that they are "not religious." But this doesn't mean that they have found a way to live without faith. It merely reveals that they have a very narrow definition of religion, such as "going to church" or "believing in God."

A much more realistic definition is offered by the Columbia Encyclopedia. "Religion," it says, "has to do with what is most vital in the feeling, belief and performance of every human being." In other words, your religion is the set of assumptions—conscious or unconscious—on which you base your day-to-day decisions and actions.

A person may try to sidestep the religious issue by saying, "I'm an agnostic . . . I just don't know what to believe." But this dodge won't work. As the great Protestant preacher Dr. Harry Emerson Fosdick has pointed out, "you can avoid making up your mind, but you cannot avoid making up your life." Each day we are confronted with decisions, alternative courses of conduct, big choices and little choices. We may wish to suspend judgment on the ultimate meaning of human existence, but in actual fact we find ourselves compelled to act as if certain things were true and certain values more important than others. In every showdown, great or petty, we bet our lives on some hypothesis about God.

I say *hypothesis* to underscore the role that faith plays in all religious decisions, even those that are cynical or despairing. Religion need never be irrational, but religious convictions are *always* transrational, in the sense that they necessarily involve intuitions, instincts, emotions, and perceptions, as well as rational thought. We have fallen into the custom of reserving the word "faith" for religious beliefs that affirm the existence of a deity. But this is an inaccurate way of speaking. In reality, it is just as much an act of faith to assert that the universe just happens to be here as it is to say "In the beginning God created the heaven and the earth."

Basically, there are three hypotheses about God. They are called *atheism, pantheism,* and *theism.*

The Beliefs of the Atheists

The atheist stakes all on the proposition that God is just a figment of the human imagination, a name invented by prescientific man to explain what he could not understand.

The chief articles of the atheist's creed have been summarized by the British philosopher Bertrand Russell. An atheist, he says, believes "that man is the product of causes which had no prevision of the end they were achieving; that his origin, his growth, his hopes and fears, his loves and beliefs, are but the outcome of accidental collocations of atoms; that no fire, no heroism, no intensity of thought or feeling, can preserve an individual life beyond the grave; that all the labors of the ages, all the devotion, all the inspiration, all the noonday brightness of human genius, are destined to extinction in the vast death of the solar system."

A negative conviction, however strongly held, is of little help as a guide to daily living. A person who disbelieves in God is compelled to decide what he *does* believe in, or he will have no criteria by which to make the choices and decisions that crowd in on him daily.

Hedonism: Faith in Pleasure

Many atheists find their positive affirmations in the attitude toward life called *hedonism*. The name comes from the Greek word for pleasure, and its intellectual ancestry traces back to the Greek philosophers, particularly Epicurus. The hedonist believes that enjoyment is the chief end of human existence. His creed is perfectly expressed in the ancient aphorism, "Eat, drink and be merry, for tomorrow you may die." The modern version is, "Live it up while you can; you're a long time dead."

Hedonists have never seen fit to organize a church, or otherwise institutionalize their faith. In fact, many of them find it expedient to pay lip service to other religious creeds and maintain nominal ties with churches that enjoy a high degree of prestige in the community. For this reason, it is difficult to estimate how many adherents this religion has in America at present. But the number is unquestionably very large. And it is growing quite rapidly. Hedonists do not operate any Sunday schools, nor do they hold revival meetings. But they nevertheless conduct one of the most widespread and effective religious education programs of any faith. Through movies, television, newspapers, magazines, and other mass media, they spread the hedonist gospel that there is no claim on human beings higher than the gratification of the senses, and that "happiness" is the only thing that matters.

Although hedonism has a powerful attraction for young people, it seems to have trouble holding onto its converts as they grow older. "No one gets bored faster than the person who feels that his only pleasure in life is to keep himself amused," one apostate hedonist explained. Convinced that pleasure is the greatest good, the hedonist finds himself compelled to go to ever greater pains to achieve it. Like a narcotics addict, he has to keep increasing the dose to get his kicks. It is a sober fact that quite a large number of hedonists end by committing suicide. Many others eventually turn to a more demanding—and more rewarding—kind of faith.

Humanism: Faith in Man

Hedonism is sometimes called the most self-centered of all religions. At the opposite pole is another atheistic religion, which attracts unselfish, generous-spirited men and women. It is called *humanism*.

One of its leading exponents, Sir Julian Huxley, defines a humanist as "someone who believes that Man is just as much a natural phenomenon as an animal or a plant; that his body, mind and soul were not supernaturally created, but are all products of evolution, and that he is not under the control or guidance of any supernatural being or beings, but has to rely on himself and his own powers."

Although he finds nothing else in the universe to worship, the humanist has great reverence for Man (spelled, characteristically, with a capital M). He believes that Man can invest his transitory existence with meaning and dignity by creating his own values and struggling gallantly toward them in a world that is at best indifferent and at worst hostile toward his hopes.

Authentic existence can be achieved, the humanist says, by pursuing two goals. One is self-development—the realization of one's maximum potential as a human being. The other is social progress—the realization of civilization's maximum potential as a favorable environment for human aspirations.

Humanism asserts that these goals can be attained, without any kind of divine help or intervention in human affairs, through science and education. If this "religion without revelation," as Huxley calls it, can be said to have dogmas, the most important are its faith in the power of science to free Man from all the limitations that beset him, and the power of education to imbue him with high ideals, pure motivations, and self-discipline.

Humanists are only a little better organized than hedonists. A few have banded together in the *Ethical Culture Society* and *The American Humanist Association*. Some have drifted into unitarian churches (see pp. 148ff.). But the vast majority are not affiliated with any specifically religious organization (even though they may be up to their ears in civic, political, and cultural groups).

Humanism is unquestionably a far more idealistic creed than hedonism. The question is whether it is *too* idealistic. A generation that has seen Man behave as he did during the Hitler era and World War II may have legitimate doubts as to his ability to save and perfect himself. Even the tools by which Man is expected to achieve his heaven-on-earth—science and education—are no longer held in quite the awe they inspired before their joint endeavors brought humanity under the shadow of the hydrogen bomb.

Communism: Faith in Materialism

The largest and best organized of the atheistic religions is *Communism*. Some readers may be astonished to find it listed as a religion. But many close observers of the Communist movement, including FBI Director J. Edgar Hoover, have concluded that it can be understood only as a faith that demands the total allegiance of its adherents. In his authoritative study *The Nature of Communism*, Professor Robert V. Daniels says:

"The Communist Party is a sect, with beliefs, mission, priesthood and hierarchy. It is a church, in the very obvious sense that it is the institutionalization of belief. . . . Fervor, dogmatism, fanaticism, dedication, atonement and martyrdom can all be observed in the Communist movement.

"So far does the character of the Communist's allegiance to the movement correspond to religious commitment that we can even observe the intensely emotional phenomenon of conversion when individuals are persuaded to embrace the Communist faith."

been employed in whatever fashion seemed most oppor-
tune to undermine faith in God.

Although Soviet Russia clearly has some first-class brains
in its service—its space program is sufficient testimony to
their existence—they evidently have not been utilized in
formulating the government's program of atheistic propaganda. Some of the arguments used by the Russian Communists in recent years to "disprove" the existence of God
recall the late G. K. Chesterton's wry remark that he owed
his conversion to Christianity to atheists, whose flimsy
logic "aroused in my mind the first wild doubts of doubt."

For example, the official Soviet propaganda apparatus has
made a very big thing of the statement by cosmonaut
Gherman S. Titov that he looked all around for God while
orbiting the earth in his spacecraft, and—"I didn't find anyone out there."

The straight-faced emphasis given by Moscow Radio to
Titov's "discovery" suggests that there must be high-ups in
the Communist Party who really believe that if God existed
he would be readily visible to any space pilot.

This childish type of atheism is evidently not too appealing to the Russian people, who have been bombarded with
it for decades through their schools, newspapers, and broadcasting stations. Leonid Ilyichev, head of the Communist
Party's ideological commission, acknowledged in 1964 that
there was a great need for more effective preaching of the
atheist message. "The number of people practicing religious rites continues to be relatively high," he said.

Of still greater significance, perhaps, is the report of Har-
rison Salisbury, veteran New York Times correspondent
who knows modern Russia as well as any Westerner, that

The principal dogma of Communist theology i
tic materialism." As expounded in the "sacred wri
Karl Marx and V. I. Lenin, the dogma holds that
ical world of things which can be seen, felt, weig
measured is the only reality that exists. All talk
spiritual dimension to human experience is nonse

Communist dogma goes on to state that econom
—not human aspirations for freedom, nor other
ideals—are the real shapers of history. In particular,
termining factor in the evolution of society is tl
struggle—the inevitable conflict between the exploi
the exploited, the capitalists who own the tools of
tion and the workers who use them.

It is an article of faith with every devout Com
that the working out of the class struggle will eve
bring the Communist Party to power in every part
world. When that red millennium comes to pas
class struggle will cease, the Communist state will
der the dictatorial powers it has had to assume duri
struggle, and everyone will live happily ever after.

Lenin declared in one of his tracts that Comm
must always be "militantly atheistic." "All moderr
gions are instruments of bourgeois reaction that serve
fend exploitation and to drug the working class," he

The Communist Party has been in power in Russi
nearly half a century, and throughout this time it ha
lowed, with varying degrees of zeal, Lenin's prescriptic
"resolute hostility" toward all rival religions. Period
harsh and open persecution have alternated with perio
relative tolerance, but always the power of the state

"some of the most brilliant Soviet scientists" are quietly revolting against the purely materialistic concept of the universe laid down in Communist dogma.

"These men have not become believers in a formal religion or dogma," Salisbury says. "But they are no longer atheists. They believe that there must exist in the universe a force or power that is superior to any possessed by man."

The Varieties of Pantheism

Let's pause for a brief summary: We said there are three basic hypotheses about God—atheism, pantheism, theism. We first took a look at atheism—the "no God" hypothesis —and found three principal varieties currently competing in the idea market. Now let's examine the second basic hypothesis about God—pantheism.

Pantheism's distinctive belief is summed up in its name, which is a compound of the Greek words *pan* (all) and *theos* (God). To the pantheist, "God is all and all is God." In other words, he identifies God with the universe and the universe with God.

To some pantheists, God is the all-important part of the God-universe equation. They speak of the visible, temporal world as being merely "an idea in the mind of God." Others approach from the opposite direction. They speak of God as if the word were merely a synonym for nature.

In either case, the pantheist is convinced of the "oneness" of all things, and his concept of God is "the Whole that gathers up in itself all that exists." He may use the traditional word for convenience, but for him "God" is *not* a proper name. It is an abstract noun, meaning "underlying principle of unity," and it has no connotations of personhood. Pantheists do *not* believe in a God who exists apart from the natural universe as a separate, transcendent Being.

The pantheistic concept of a divinity dwelling within and indistinguishable from nature is vividly expressed in a passage from Wordsworth's poem *Tintern Abbey*:

> ". . . a sense sublime
> Of something far more deeply interfused,
> Whose dwelling is the light of setting suns,
> And the round ocean and the living air,
> And the blue sky and in the mind of man;
> A motion and a spirit, that impels
> All thinking things, all objects of all thoughts,
> And rolls through all things."

Like atheism, pantheism is an over-all term that embraces a wide variety of specific beliefs, ranging from the most primitive kind of superstition to highly sophisticated philosophical concepts.

Primitive Animism

The primitive version of pantheism is called *animism*. Animists believe that various objects, such as stones, trees, mountains, or the sun—objects we would call *inanimate*—are actually suffused with supernatural spirits who must be propitiated and cajoled. The ancestor worship of Japanese Shintoism and the spiritism of South American Indians are very closely related to animism since they entail the same idea; that is, of a natural world overrun by invisible spirits.

Although Westerners tend to think of animism as a form of belief that went out with Stone-Age man, it remains today one of the world's major religions, in terms of numbers, with more than 100 million followers in Africa, Asia, Polynesia, and South America.

Classic and Modern Polytheism

Polytheism is another variety of pantheistic religion that is still strong. Polytheists believe in many different gods. The mythologies of ancient Greece and Rome are classic examples of polytheism. Both acknowledged one chief deity— the Greeks called him Zeus; the Romans, Jupiter. But his control over the universe was regarded as quite limited; other gods and goddesses were free to do pretty much as they pleased in the particular realms of nature or human activity over which they held jurisdiction. Thus, in the Roman pantheon, Mars had charge of war, Apollo took care of the sun, Neptune ruled the ocean, Ceres had the last word in agriculture, Diana in hunting, and Venus in love. Altogether, the Greeks and Romans recognized about thirty thousand gods.

In the modern world, we encounter polytheism mainly in the Oriental religions. Later we shall devote a whole chapter to these ancient faiths, which have more than 700 million adherents in Asia. But it is pertinent here to note that Hinduism is based on a pantheistic view of the universe and that in popular practice it is extremely polytheistic. By one reckoning, Hinduism has about 3 million gods —a hundred times as many as the ancient Greeks and Romans! Buddhism, an offshoot of Hinduism, is not so easily categorized. Some versions of Buddhism—those that have remained closest to the spirit of its founder, Gautama Buddha—are really more atheistic than pantheistic. But there are other types of Buddhism—the ones with the largest followings in Asia today—that have degenerated into polytheistic idol worship.

Far removed from either animism or polytheism is the pantheism of poets and philosophers, which is reflected in the lines of Wordsworth quoted above. The sages of India were the first to develop the idea that individual existence is merely an illusion, and that all persons and things are simply waves on an infinite sea of being. Their concept of all-embracing unity is spelled out in the Upanishads, the Vedas, and other sacred writings that date back thousands of years.

Spinoza, Emerson, and the Bishop of Woolwich

There is also a long and respectable pantheistic tradition in Western philosophy, beginning with the Greek Stoics and Neoplatonists.

Perhaps the greatest Western exponent of pantheism was the eighteenth-century Dutch philosopher Baruch Spinoza. Spinoza held that "all existence is embraced in one substance—God," and that the world of nature is "but a manifestation of God"—in fact, is God. Spinoza traced this hypothesis to its logical conclusions, pointing out that it left no room whatever for any ideas about chance, free will, or the immortality of individual souls. On the other hand, he noted, it provided a perfect answer for the seemingly insoluble problem of why a good God should permit evil in his creation. Evil, said Spinoza, exists only from the viewpoint of a finite creature who has the "illusion" of separate existence. It does not exist when seen as part of the seamless whole of infinite, eternal reality.

In the nineteenth century, America produced a distinguished pantheist in Ralph Waldo Emerson. Emerson's attachment to Hindu concepts of "oneness" is reflected in all his writings, most notably in a poem entitled *Brahma* which includes the familiar lines:

> "They reckon ill who leave me out,
> I am the doubter—and the doubt."

Coming down to our own century, pantheistic ideas are reflected in the work of Edward Caird, R. J. Campbell, and other members of the British-American school of philosophy known as "absolute idealism." Some readers detect more than a whiff of pantheism in the writings of the famed American theologian Paul Tillich, who insists that God must not be thought of as "*a* Being" but rather as "the infinite and inexhaustible depth and ground of all being." And at least one of Tillich's would-be interpreters, Dr. John A. T. Robinson, Bishop of Woolwich, England, got himself so deeply entangled in pantheism in his controversial book *Honest to God* that he found it necessary to tack on a final chapter in which he declared, more vigorously than convincingly, that he was not either a pantheist.

The Faith in One God

Theism (or, as some prefer to say, *monotheism*) is professed by about 1.5 billion people—half of the world's population. This concept of God is shared by Christians, Jews, and Moslems.

Theists are united in several affirmations about the nature of God. One is expressed succinctly in the Shema Yisrael, which Jews recite at every religious service and, if possible, at the hour of death: "Hear, O Israel, the Lord our God, the Lord is One." It is echoed in the creed that every devout Moslem repeats five times a day: "There is no God but Allah." To a person who has grown up in a Christian culture, the assertion that there is only one God may sound trite and obvious. But both Judaism and Islam—the correct name for the Moslems' religion—grew up in the midst of polytheistic cultures. When the Jews and Moslems declared that there was one God, and one only, they were making a radical contradiction of what most of the people around them had always believed.

A second basic belief that is common to all theists is that God is *both immanent and transcendent.* To describe God as immanent is to say, with the pantheists, that He dwells within nature and particularly within the hearts and minds of men. To call Him transcendent is to say, in direct opposition to pantheism, that He is also beyond and above, utterly independent of the material universe which He has called into being, and "wholly other" than any created thing.

Theists also agree in ascribing to God the attributes of personhood. This does *not* mean taking an anthropomorphic view of God as a grandfatherly Being who exists somewhere "out there" in space. On the contrary, theistic scholars are the first to insist that God cannot properly be conceived as a particular thing, not even as "the highest person" or "the Supreme Being." Theism's God is infinitely more than a person or *a* being. He is *the* Source of all personhood, existence, and reality, totally beyond the powers of man to comprehend or describe.

Since God transcends any of the categories of human intelligence into which we may try to fit Him, the only question is whether we do less injustice to His majesty by referring to Him in personal pronouns, or by using impersonal abstract nouns, such as "Ground of Being" and "First Cause."

Pantheists have a strong preference for use of abstractions. So do some other people who have never studied pantheistic doctrines, but who have the feeling that a polysyllabic phrase sounds much more scientific and intellectual than a simple name like "God."

The Personal God

Theists speak of God in categories appropriate to personhood for two reasons. First, they believe that personality —thinking, willing, purposeful personality—is by far the highest form of existence that we have encountered in this complex universe. Therefore, it is the least inadequate frame of reference in which to speak of, or to, God. The second reason is more basic and more empirical. In their experience of God, Christians, Jews, and Moslems have been certain that they were dealing, not with an It, but with a Thou.

And that brings us to the fourth fundamental conviction of the theistic religions. God desires to enter into a personal, I-Thou relationship with His human creatures. He loves them ("as tenderly as a mother bird loves her young," say the Moslem scriptures, the Koran) and He takes the initiative in revealing Himself to them.

The concept of a self-revealing God is one of the great practical, as well as theoretical, points of difference between pantheists and theists. The pantheist feels that it is up to him to gain such knowledge of God, or—to use a term more congenial to him—Ultimate Reality, as he can. He tends to be eclectic in his quest for wisdom, borrowing one idea from the Bible and another from the Bhagavad-Gita. But Christianity, Judaism, and Islam are "religions of revelation." They place their faith not in any human speculation about what God *ought* to be like, but in what they believe He has revealed about Himself. So they naturally accord great importance to the particular sacred writings, or scriptures, in which they believe God's self-revelation is authentically recorded. Islamic scholars refer to Moslems, Jews, and Christians as "people of the Book," and the phrase aptly depicts one of the most profound bonds among the theistic religions.

CHAPTER II

The Jewish-Christian Heritage

There are in the world today some 12 million people whose very existence is one of the most remarkable facts of history.

These people are the Jews. By birth, marriage, or adoption in faith, they are all members of a single family—a family that traces its genealogy back nearly four thousand years to a Middle Eastern nomad named Abraham.

The survival of this family as a self conscious entity through forty centuries would be enough in itself to make the Jews a unique people. No other human family approaches it in size or antiquity. But the descendants of Abraham have survived much more than time. They have endured the most ruthless and long-continued persecution ever visited upon any people. They have clung to their family identity no matter how high the price—and that price has ranged from living in ghettoes to dying in gas chambers.

The mystery does not end there. For the Jews have not merely kept alive. They have placed an indelible mark on human civilization, and particularly on the moral and religious life of mankind. Out of this people came two of the

world's great theistic religions—Judaism and Christianity.*
Our purpose in this chapter is to examine these two
Jewish faiths to see what they have in common and wherein
they differ.

The description of Christianity as a Jewish faith may
shock some Christians—and probably some Jews as well.
After two thousand years of bitter estrangement and mutual contempt, both Jews and Christians are inclined to
forget how closely they are bound together by common
beliefs and a common history. But the relationship
remains an intimate one, however little it may be acknowledged on either side. It is not simply a matter of
Jesus being a Jew. *All* the people who founded the Christian Church were Jews. And they had no intention of
starting a "new" religion. For them, Christianity was a
fulfillment rather than a repudiation of Judaism. It built
upon, and took for granted, the Jewish religious heritage,
and its essential doctrines would be quite meaningless
apart from that context.

The implication of these facts—which are clearly set
forth in the New Testament—is that no one can become
a Christian without also becoming in some sense a Jew.
That is what the late Pope Pius XII meant when he said,
"Spiritually, we are Semites."

The Vision of Abraham

The almost incredible story of the Jews begins with a
religious vision experienced by a seventy-five-year-old patriarch who lived about 2000 B.C. in the city of Ur. Ur was

---

* Islam also traces its spiritual ancestry back to Abraham, but not
through the Jews. We shall go into this in Chapter IX.

even then a very old city. It lay in the middle of the "cradle of civilization," the rich valley of Mesopotamia between the Tigris and Euphrates rivers.

The patriarch was Abraham. The little we know about him comes from the ancient family history recorded in Genesis, the first book of the Bible. But it is sufficient to establish him as a man of uncommon faith and courage.

Abraham lived in a polytheistic, idol-worshipping culture. There is no clear evidence that he personally ever attained the high concept of monotheism which his children were destined to develop and pass along to mankind. Abraham may have thought of his God, whom he called Jehovah, as the greatest of many deities. There is at least a hint of this in very early Hebrew poetry, which refers to Jehovah as "a great King above all gods." At any rate, Abraham was willing to bet his life on Jehovah.

Jehovah put Abraham's faith to a severe test.

"Go from your country and your kindred and your father's house to the land that I will show you," He commanded, "and I will make of you a great nation . . . and by you all the families of the earth will be blessed."

Abraham went. At an age when men are reluctant to risk new adventures, he pulled up stakes, severed all ties with home and family, and set forth with his wife Sarah for the Promised Land, then called Canaan, which later became known as Palestine. This act of obedience to God by an obscure man was one of the most important events in the religious history of the human race.

Abraham and Sarah were childless, and Sarah had already experienced menopause. She shrugged off with a bitter laugh Abraham's assurances that Jehovah would make them the progenitors of a whole nation of people. But at the age of ninety Sarah became pregnant and bore a son whom she named Isaac.

Isaac followed in his father's footsteps as a nomadic sheepherder. He had a son named Jacob. (Jacob later acquired a new name, Israel; hence the terms "children of Israel," and "Israelites" for his descendants.)

During Jacob's old age, a severe famine drove the family out of Palestine and into Egypt. There the Israelites remained for several centuries. They vastly increased in number but retained close ties of kinship. Instead of becoming assimilated into the Egyptian population and adopting the Egyptian gods, they clung doggedly to their identity as a separate people, and continued to worship the God of Abraham, Isaac, and Jacob. Their status as a foreign enclave within Egypt gradually deteriorated into a condition of slavery.

Moses and the Chosen People

About 1200 B.C., the oppressed Israelites acquired a leader who was as full of faith and courage as his forefather Abraham. His name was Moses, one of the greatest leaders of all time. The second book of the Bible, Exodus, describes vividly how Moses led his people out of captivity with the help of "mighty acts of God." The pact, or covenant, that Jehovah had made with Abraham was renewed with Moses:

"If you will obey My voice and keep My covenant, you

shall be My own possession among all peoples. . . . you shall be to Me a kingdom of priests and a holy nation."

The Jewish scriptures tell how Moses communed with God on the top of Mount Sinai, and returned with the tablets of stone on which were inscribed the Ten Commandments, which have served for more than three thousand years as the basic moral code of the Judaeo-Christian civilization. In addition to laws of a moral nature, Moses laid down detailed rules on food-handling and diet, the observance of religious rites, and the regulation of all kinds of human relationships, from that of husband and wife to that of master and servant. This vast and complex body of legislation fills a large part of the first five books of the Bible, which are known to Jews as the Torah, or the Law.

Many Gentiles resent the idea of the Jews being God's "chosen people"; they consider it an arrogant claim. There may even lurk in some Gentile breasts a conviction that the persecutions that the Jews have suffered are a sort of come-uppance for being so presumptuous.

But it was not with any sense of self-righteousness or of racial superiority that the children of Israel entered into their "covenant" with God. Their feelings about the matter are accurately expressed in Dorothy Parker's famed couplet:

"How odd of God
To choose the Jews."

They were mystified that God, with all the great civilizations of antiquity to choose from, should select a slave-people to be His "holy nation." Their amazement shows through very clearly in the records they left behind, which we now call Scripture.

Moreover, the Jews understood from the start that there was a *quid pro quo* involved in the covenant. Their part of the bargain was to obey God's laws, as transmitted to them by Moses. Their recognition of the heavy burden they accepted is reflected in a very old Jewish legend which says that God offered the Torah to every tribe and nation on earth, but only the Jews were willing to put on the yoke of obedience.

Israel did not wear the yoke joyously. The history of the Jews, recorded with such fascinating candor in the Old Testament, is that of a stiff-necked people who were always rebelling against the discipline of the Torah and turning their backs on God. They often resented the covenant, and instead of reveling in their unique role as a chosen people, wanted God to go away and leave them alone.

But God would not do that. Sometimes, when His chosen people grew particularly unruly, He would chastise them severely. Often He sent prophets like Isaiah, Amos, and Jeremiah to castigate them for their willfulness and disobedience. But He never abandoned His covenant with them. "I will punish you in just measure," He said through Jeremiah, "but I will not make a full end of you." Instead of despairing of them, he made them a new promise:

"Behold the days are coming when I shall make a new covenant with the House of Israel . . . I will put my law within them, and write it upon their hearts, and I will be their God and they shall be my people . . . for I will forgive their iniquity and remember their sin no more."

Jesus of Nazareth

From Jeremiah and other great prophets, the Jews learned that God would some day send a Very Special Person—an "anointed one" (in Hebrew, *mahsiah*, "Messiah")—who as their leader would put everything right, and establish the rule of God among all peoples. Anticipation of the Messiah's coming gradually developed into a major element of Jewish faith, a hope that sustained the Hebrews through hard times, exile, and suffering.

Twelve centuries after the children of Israel escaped from bondage in Egypt and embarked upon their stormy career as God's "holy nation," there appeared among them an extraordinary person, named Jesus of Nazareth.

The story of Jesus is told in an ancient collection of short books and letters, written, for the most part, by men who had known him in person. These writings have been preserved by the Christian Church as the New Testament of the Bible. They can hardly be called an unbiased record since they were written by men who had a definite viewpoint about Jesus. On the other hand, they have been subjected to the most exhaustive scholarly scrutiny ever focused on any documents. Nothing has been taken for granted: every conceivable doubt about the authenticity of any aspect of the story has been raised and debated at length. This skeptical shakedown of the New Testament has not settled all questions about what really happened in connection with certain events that some scholars regard as myth, others as historical fact. But the net result has been to confirm the essential historicity of the story of

Jesus to a degree that has frankly surprised some of the savants who have participated in the quest.

The story of Jesus has been recounted so often and so well in other books—and best of all in the New Testament —that it need not be repeated here in any detail. It is sufficient to note that he came from very humble origins— a carpenter's family in an obscure village; that he attracted no particular public attention during the first thirty years of his life; and that he then set forth to proclaim the advent of the "Kingdom of God"—the rule of God on earth which the prophets had said would be established by the Messiah.

His career as an itinerant preacher was fairly brief—no more than three years, possibly only one year. But it had a tremendous impact on the people of Palestine. Jesus became known far and wide as one who "went about doing good"—healing the sick, comforting the sorrowful, challenging the complacent, sharing the deprivations of the poor. No one in the past two thousand years has been able to read the New Testament accounts of what he did and said without feeling an attraction to this incredibly empathetic, witty, understanding, self-giving, fiercely honest person who seemed to love all sorts and conditions of men, even those who wronged him.

There is no evidence that Jesus ever claimed, in so many words, to be the Messiah. Perhaps he felt that the title had acquired too many connotations of earthly kingship. What he did say, boldly and repeatedly, was that he had been sent by "my Father in Heaven" to show men the way, to tell them the truth, and to make it possible for them to enter into authentic, abundant life.

Did the Jews Reject Jesus?

The common people "heard him gladly," and followed him around in ever-growing throngs. It is worth emphasizing that these common people—who were the first to accept and respond to the message of Jesus—were Jews. This should be borne in mind whenever you hear someone speak glibly about "the Jews" rejecting Jesus.

The Jews who rejected Jesus were the "big shots" of the community—the "Establishment" of religious, political, and civic leaders. They had reason to dislike him, since he constantly took them to task for their hypocrisy and self-righteousness. But their real grievance against him was that he was rocking the boat—"stirring up the people," as they put it—challenging the *status quo.* There is no question about Jesus' guilt on this charge: he *was* a radical, and he *did* start a revolution which was to shake the foundations not only of the society of his day but of every subsequent society that has tried to ignore his proclamation that all human beings are equally and infinitely precious in the sight of God.

The Establishment had Jesus arrested. He was tried before a religious court, and convicted of blasphemy for claiming a special relationship with God. He was then turned over to Pontius Pilate, the Roman governor (Palestine was then a Roman province). Pilate ordered Jesus put to death by crucifixion, the most horrible form of execution that the callous Romans had been able to devise; the sentence was carried out on a hill named Golgotha just outside Jerusalem on a spring day in the year A.D. 30.

As he hung on the cross, dying slowly from sheer agony, he said, "Father, forgive them, for they know not what they do."

The Dazzling Light of the Resurrection

His disciples had scattered in terror after Jesus' arrest. Some went back to their native Galilee; others went into hiding in Jerusalem. Although Jesus had dropped many cryptic hints to the effect that his death would not be the final chapter in the story, it is obvious from their own shamefaced accounts of their conduct that the disciples had not taken him seriously. He was dead, ignominiously dead, and once his body had been buried in a hastily borrowed sepulchre, the disciples never expected to see him again.

But they did see him again. At least, they said they did. And they stuck by their story through ridicule and torture, and even when they had to choose between recantation and death.

Some people reject the story of the Resurrection on the ground that human experience testifies overwhelmingly to the finality of death. Jesus couldn't have risen from the dead, they say, because things like that just don't happen. To which Christians may reply: "But that is precisely the point. The Resurrection *was* an extraordinary event, which assures us more forcibly than anything else could that Jesus really was a Very Special Person."

In the dazzling light of the Resurrection experience, the disciples, and especially that brilliant Johnny-come-lately,

Paul, rethought the things Jesus had done and said during his ministry, the effect he had had on their lives, and the clues he had dropped concerning his identity.

They came to the conclusion that Jesus was not only the long-expected Messiah (in Greek, *Christos*, "Christ"), but also "the Son of God." In this title, they sought to express their conviction that Jesus, while fully and completely human, was at the same time God Incognito, or, as one of the Gospels puts it, "the Word of God made flesh."

They also concluded that Jesus' death on the cross was an act of atonement, not for any wrongs that he had done, but for the sins of other men—all men of all ages. By his willingness to suffer even unto death for the sake of others, including those who despised him, Jesus had achieved once and for all the triumph of love over evil, and had established the "new covenant" that God had promised through Jeremiah (p. 26).

Included in the promise of the new covenant was the statement "I will put my law within them, and write it upon their hearts." This was fulfilled, Christians believe, when the visible presence of Christ was succeeded by the invisible but strongly felt presence of the Holy Spirit, who comes to man as "God within," providing guidance, strength, and irresistible inward testimony to the reality of God and the truth of Christ.

We have barely scratched the surface of Jewish history and Christian theology in this brief summary, and I hope you'll investigate both subjects further by reading some of the more detailed books recommended in the last section of this book. Our purpose here is simply to identify the main beliefs which Jews and Christians share, and the principal points on which they differ.

Jewish and Christian Concepts

The most basic thing which Jews and Christians have in common is their concept of God. Some Christians have the mistaken impression that Jews believe in a harsh, avenging, legalistic God, who bears little resemblance to the merciful Father in Heaven revealed by Jesus. But Jesus did not radically alter the picture of God that had been painted by the great prophets and psalmists (whose scriptures he read, revered, and often quoted). What Jesus did was to pick out of the vast treasury of Jewish religious thought those insights which, he said, came closest to the truth about God, and to discard other ideas which he held to be false, misleading, or unworthy. In some of his parables—such as the one about the prodigal son—he seems to go further than any Jewish teacher had ever gone before in depicting God as One who is not only willing but eager to be reconciled with sinful man. But on the whole, the God whom men have encountered in the life and teaching of Christ is recognizably the same as the righteous, yet loving Jehovah who spoke through Isaiah.

This Jewish-Christian God is *personal*, not in any naïvely anthropomorphic sense, but in the all-important sense of being One who cares, purposes, and communicates. He is a God who *acts* within history, and who makes Himself known to men through His acts. He cares nothing for empty ritual and outward shows of reverence, but

He is intensely concerned with justice, and He expects men to show kindness, generosity, and love in their dealings with one another.

The basic difference between Jews and Christians is their attitude toward Jesus.

Changing Attitudes

Until a comparatively few years ago, most Jews hated the very name of Jesus. And small wonder. For hundreds of years, Jews had been subjected to merciless treatment by persecutors who claimed to be acting in Jesus' name. In our own day, there has been a belated and as yet inadequate recognition by Christians that nothing could be further from the spirit of Christ than to despise Jews. Both Protestants and Roman Catholics have taken steps to purge their religious-education materials of passages that might encourage Christian children to grow up with the warped notion that Jews are "Christ-killers" who deserve to suffer. They have placed new emphasis on what has always been orthodox Christian doctrine, but which has not always been made clear in Christian teaching: that *all* men share the guilt for the crucifixion, because it was for the sins of *all* men in *all ages* that Christ died.

Partly in response to this more Christian attitude on the part of Christians, and partly on their own initiative, Jews have begun to take another look at Jesus. Norman Cousins, the distinguished Jewish editor of *Saturday Review*, has urged Jews to "take pride in Jesus the Jew." "No other figure—spiritual, philosophical, political, or intellectual—has had a greater impact on human history," Cousins said.

Rabbi Maurice N. Eisendrath, president of the Union of American Hebrew Congregations, also has challenged Jews to "render unto Jesus that which is Jesus'" and to acknowledge that "his influence was a beneficial one, not only to the pagans but to the Jews of his time as well."

These ironic comments should not be mistaken by Christians as evidence that Rabbi Eisendrath or Mr. Cousins or other Jews are now ripe for conversion. However far the leaders of modern Judaism may go in reclaiming Jesus as a Jew, they continue to look upon him as strictly a human person. The belief that Jesus was God Incarnate, which is the linchpin of the Christian faith, is to a devout Jew pure blasphemy.

Jews who are traditional in their religious views believe that the promised Messiah is still to come. Some, more liberal in theology, have abandoned the expectation of a personal Messiah, and speak instead of a "Messianic age." There is general agreement, however, that when the Messiah or Messianic age does come, the evils that beset humankind will vanish and men will live together in peace, justice, and joy under the reign of God.

Since that golden age has plainly not yet arrived, Jews say, Jesus could not have been the Messiah.

Christians say that Jesus *has* "made all things new" for those who open their hearts to him, and permit his spirit to rule their lives. His kingdom may not be readily apparent to the world at large, for it exists within men and there are still a great many people (including some who loudly profess his name) who have not accepted his lordship. The fulfillment of the messianic hope for a complete transformation and redemption of human society must await the time when Christ will come again, this time not incognito as a carpenter, but in the full glory of the Son of God.

The sharp divergence of Jewish and Christian views on Jesus is reflected in other theological differences between Judaism and Christianity, particularly on the question of what men must do to be saved.

Must Man Save Himself?

Judaism is more concerned with deeds than beliefs. It teaches that man does not need a saviour: that he can justify himself before God by obeying the Law of the Torah. "Jews believe," says Rabbi Arthur Gilbert, "that man can and does fulfill his responsibility to God by living as creatively and as righteously and as sanctified a life as possible here and now in this world."

Christianity asserts that men are weak and self-centered creatures who are unable to live up to even the milder demands of the Law, let alone obey the Great Commandment to "love the Lord thy God with all thy heart, and thy neighbor as thyself." If man had only his own righteousness to speak for him, he would never be worthy to face God. But man does not have to save himself. Jesus has already accomplished man's salvation through one mighty act of self-giving and obedience which outweighs in the scales of divine judgment all the sins of the human race through all of history. Christians believe that God could not simply overlook our sins or pretend they were unimportant: to do so would have made a mockery of His moral law. What He could do, and did in Christ, was to bear for us the pain and humiliation which we deserved to suffer, and thereby made it possible for us to come home to Him. "By God's grace you are saved, through faith," said the Apostle Paul. "It is not our doing, but God's free gift."

Evangelism and Conversion

Should Christians try to convert Jews—or vice versa? This is a perennial topic for debate among theologians. Jews have traditionally shown little interest in winning converts. This reflects their conviction that what a man believes is not nearly so important as how he lives. "Jews do not believe that they must convert others in order to achieve the redemption of humankind," says Rabbi Gilbert. "Let each nation, each people, all religions, come to God, each in their own way."

Christianity, by contrast, has always been an intensely evangelistic religion. Its compulsion to bring all men to Christ reflects its conviction that He is "the Way, the Truth and the Life," and that "there is no other name under heaven whereby men can be saved." But there has also been a persistent belief among Christian thinkers— from St. Paul through Reinhold Niebuhr—that the Jews are a special case, and that God perhaps has reasons for keeping the Old Israel intact instead of letting it be absorbed into the "New Israel" of the Christian Church. This viewpoint is rejected by Christians who believe that the great mission for which the Jews were chosen—as lightbearers to mankind—was fulfilled with the coming of Christ.

"Jesus Christ came first to the Jews," says the Reverend Reynolds N. Johnson, evangelism director of the Lutheran Church in America. "His church must never fail to include Jews in its concern, witness and welcome."

So far as most Jews are concerned, the question is academic. Dr. Gerson Cohen, professor of Jewish history at Columbia University, says that Jews have many differences about religion, but there is one "strong though negative tie linking Jews throughout the world." It is "the refusal to convert to Christianity."

Orthodox, Conservative, and Reform Judaism

The religious differences among Jews, to which Dr. Cohen refers, are sharper than most outsiders realize. Denominational rivalries are every bit as keen in Judaism as in Protestantism. The three principal denominations are known as Orthodox, Conservative, and Reform.

Orthodox Jews are the most numerous, both in the United States and in Israel. They believe that all the Mosaic laws—including the dietary and Sabbath observance regulations—are still strictly binding. (Anyone who thinks that Orthodox Judaism is a fossil faith, taken seriously only by a few grey-bearded rabbis, should read Herman Wouk's book *This Is My God*, a moving testimonial of what it means to be an Orthodox Jew in twentieth-century America.)

Reform Judaism (known in Europe as Liberal Judaism) seeks to preserve the basic moral precepts of the Torah and other ethical aspects of Jewish tradition—including a passionate concern for social justice. But it holds that the dietary laws, Sabbath observance rules, and ritual regulations of the Torah may be modified, or set aside, to adjust to the circumstances of modern life. For example: in Reform temples men and women sit together, which Orthodox Jews regard as a grave violation of Mosaic law.

Conservative Jews don't like to be described as the in-between group, but they inevitably are, because the best and simplest way to define the Conservative position is to say that it is more strict than Reform and less strict than Orthodoxy.

Although Jewish unity seems at least as remote as Christian unity, there have been some evidences in recent years of an ecumenical movement in Judaism. It is motivated in part by a growing realization that the big religious question for many Jews is not whether to be Orthodox, Conservative, or Reform, but whether to abandon all of them. A very large proportion of the world's Jews—perhaps more than half—are today so thoroughly secularized that they look upon the Torah as a historic relic not worth arguing about. If they hold a Seder in their homes on the first night of the Passover, or take their families to a synagogue on the Day of Atonement, it is only because they feel that it won't do the children any harm, and may even do them a mite of good, to be exposed to a sentimental observance of old folk customs that are part of their heritage.

Some Jews who turn their backs on Judaism wind up in the Unitarian-Universalist Association (see Chapter VIII). But the typical secular Jew does not form any new religious attachments. He simply ignores the whole subject. If you ask him what his beliefs are, he'll tell you that he doesn't have any.

Who Is a Jew?

The emergence of a large body of secular Jews who can only be classified religiously as theists raises anew a question that Jewish scholars have been debating for thousands of years. Is Jewishness a matter of religion . . . of ethnic origin . . . or what?

The American Council for Judaism, a small but articulate anti-Zionist organization, insists that a person becomes a Jew by voluntarily embracing a particular religious faith, and ceases to be a Jew if and when he abandons that faith. It holds that all ethnic definitions of Jewishness ultimately play into the hands of racist bigots like Hitler.

But most Jewish organizations define Jewishness in terms of "peoplehood"—that is, a person is a Jew if he is identified, by birth, by marriage, or by his own choice, with the incredible human family that traces its ancestry back to Abraham. According to this definition, the religion of Judaism is an important part of the heritage of this people, but adherence to Judaism is not the only criterion for determining who is a Jew. As a practical matter, Jews are prepared to accept as a Jew a person who repudiates Judaism—so long as he does *not* become a Christian. This long-held popular attitude was elevated to the status of law a few years ago when the Supreme Court of Israel refused to grant Israeli citizenship to a Roman Catholic monk who claimed that he was eligible for it under a law authorizing citizenship for all Jews. The monk pointed out that both his parents were Jewish and that he had been reared as a Jew prior to his conversion. But the Court held that when he embraced Christianity, he ceased to be a Jew.

CHAPTER III

The Catholic-Protestant Differences

During the past few years, peace seems to have broken out in the cold war among Christians. In spite of a dramatic improvement in relations, however, there is still a widespread tendency for Protestants to think of Roman Catholicism as an entirely different religion. And many Catholics speak of Protestantism as though it were as alien to their own faith as Shintoism.

There *are* differences between Catholics and Protestants —real, stubborn, important differences that do not result from mere misunderstandings or semantic confusion. But ecumenical theologians who are wrestling with these differences have been impressed with another fact which deserves prior emphasis. They have discovered, in the words of Father Hans Küng, that "what unites Catholics and Protestants as Christians is incomparably more vast than what separates them."

The great bond between Catholics and Protestants, which no amount of disagreement can sever, is that both acknowledge Jesus Christ as their Lord and Saviour. They also share the basic theological affirmations of Christianity that are spelled out in the New Testament and the ancient creeds. These affirmations were outlined in the preceding chapter. They include belief in the Incarnation, the Atonement, and the Resurrection.*

Catholics and Protestants have other doctrines that are derived from, or related to, their common faith in Jesus Christ. For example, both acknowledge the continuing presence of the Holy Spirit in the Christian community. Both look upon the Bible as a divinely inspired book through whose pages the authentic Word of God can be heard afresh by every generation. Both believe in the forgiveness of sins, the efficacy of baptism, the power of prayer, and the promise of everlasting life to those who place their trust in Christ. The list might be extended indefinitely, but the longer it got, the greater would become the necessity of using vague, general language. When we begin to get specific, we find that Catholics and Protestants often mean different things even when they use the same words.

Grace and Faith—Different Meanings

Take, for instance, the word *grace*, which is sometimes called the most important single word in the Christian vocabulary. Catholics think of grace as a supernatural power which God dispenses, primarily through the Church and its sacraments, to purify the souls of naturally sinful human beings, and render them capable of holiness. Father John Walsh, S.J., has succinctly expressed the cru-

---

* These basic Christian beliefs also are shared by the third great branch of Christendom, the Eastern Orthodox communion, whose history and distinctive characteristics are reviewed in Chapter IX.

cial importance that Catholics attach to grace thus understood. "If a man dies with it in his soul, he is infallibly saved," says Father Walsh. "If he lacks it, he is infallibly lost."

When Protestants speak of grace, they usually have an entirely different concept in mind. In the words of the noted Lutheran theologian Dr. Jaroslav Pelikan, grace is "not something in man which wins God's good will, but something in God which makes man pleasing to Him." To put it differently, Protestants think of grace as an attribute *of* God rather than a gift *from* God. It is a shorthand term signifying God's determination to love, forgive, and save His human children, however little they deserve it.

Another key word in the Christian lexicon which has sharply different meanings for Catholics and Protestants is *faith*. In Catholic usage, faith means giving full and unreserved assent to doctrines that have been defined by the Church as divinely revealed truth. It is almost, if not quite, a synonym for *belief*. But to Protestants, faith is, in Martin Luther's phrase, a "reckless confidence" in the goodness of God. It is more a matter of placing your trust *in* God than of believing certain propositions *about* God.

Much more than semantics is involved here. It would be no exaggeration to say that the whole Protestant Reformation grew out of the differing definitions of grace and faith outlined above.

Luther and other Protestant reformers believed that medieval Catholicism had degraded grace by treating it as a sort of magical commodity on which the Church enjoyed a monopoly of distribution. Through control over the "channels of grace"—that is, the rites and sacraments of the Church—a corrupt and often immoral hierarchy could blackmail the rest of the human race, from kings to peasants, by saying, in effect: "If you don't do as I say, I'll cut off your supply of grace and you'll be eternally damned."

To Luther, a devout Augustinian friar who wanted to reform rather than split the Church, this crass merchandising of salvation was directly contrary to the plain teaching of the New Testament. He cited the words of St. Paul to show that salvation is a free gift which a gracious God bestows on men through Jesus Christ, without their doing anything to merit or deserve it. "Justification by grace through faith alone" became the slogan of the Reformation, and it has remained the cardinal principle of Protestant theology until this day.

During the Counter Reformation of the sixteenth century, the Catholic Church eliminated many of the gross abuses, such as the sale of indulgences, that had laid the Church open to the charge of "peddling" salvation. It also took steps to repudiate any suggestion that a man can earn his passage to heaven by pious deeds. Since the Council of Trent (1545 to 1563), it has been official Catholic teaching that sinful human beings are justified in the eyes of God —that is, saved—by faith *plus* good works. "For Catholics, quite as much as for Protestants, the whole Christian life rests on faith," says Albert Cardinal Meyer, Catholic Archbishop of Chicago. "Without faith, the 'works,' or actions, of Christian living would be without Christian value. Faith, however, itself cannot be the source of man's salvation unless it is a *living faith*, that is a faith which flowers in hope and love, and hence in the works of a Christian life of service to God and neighbor."

Few if any Protestants would take exception to that statement. In fact, it recalls Luther's remark that "good works do not make a man good, but a good man doeth good works."

If Protestants and Catholics are moving somewhat closer together on justification, they are still as far apart as ever on the other great bone of contention that figured in the Reformation split. This is the question of authority.

The Authority of the Bishops

The Catholic view of authority is clear and forthright. It goes like this: Before concluding his ministry on earth, Jesus established the Church to preserve his teachings and carry on his work among men. He gave the Apostles full power over the Church, and within the "college" of Apostles, he vested supreme authority in St. Peter. To make sure that his message could never be lost or distorted, Christ sent the Holy Spirit to protect the Church from error. This protection is so effective that the Church's formal pronouncements on essential matters of faith and morals are considered infallible; hence they must be accepted as tantamount to the very words of God.

Catholics also believe that duly consecrated bishops in every generation are "successors" to the original Apostles, and inherit all their powers. Particularly they assert that St. Peter's supreme authority has passed down to his successors as Bishop of Rome, or Pope. (The term "pope" is simply an anglicization of the Italian *Il Papa*, an affectionate synonym for "Father," which the Romans traditionally use in speaking of their bishop.)

The Second Vatican Council spent six weeks in the fall of 1963 discussing the Catholic doctrine of authority, with particular reference to the relationship between the other bishops and the Pope. In a historic vote, on October 30, 1963, the Council Fathers asserted by an overwhelming majority their conviction that the whole "college" of bishops has a right—not by sufferance but by the mandate of Christ—to share with the Pope in the exercise of supreme authority in the Church. This is the famous doctrine of collegiality that caused Council conservatives to protest bitterly that the whole concept of papal supremacy was being undermined.

Actually, the Council majority was simply trying to restore the Church's classic view of authority, and correct an excessive emphasis on papal prerogatives which has characterized Catholic theology during the past four hundred years. As the late Father Gustave Weigel perceptively observed at the time of the 1963 vote, what the Council said, in effect, was that "the government of the Church is an oligarchy, not an absolute monarchy."

In asserting the doctrine of collegiality, the Council Fathers took pains to reiterate that the Pope remains supreme, and can do on his own authority anything that he could do in union with his fellow bishops. This specifically includes the promulgation of "infallible" dogmas.

The Catholic concept of authority has the great advantage of providing a clear-cut answer to the question When Christians disagree about the teaching of Christ or the will of God, who has the last word? This is a question that Protestantism has never settled.

But Protestants find many other grounds for rejecting an authoritarian hierarchy headed by an infallible Pope.

Many Protestants balk at the primary Catholic claim that Jesus conceived of his Church as a single, highly organized, centrally governed institution. They say that the New Testament nowhere speaks of such a church, but only of different local churches, united in an informal bond of Christian fellowship.

"Upon This Rock . . ."

Sooner or later, the argument always comes around to certain words addressed by Jesus to St. Peter after the latter made his famous confession of faith: "Thou art the Christ. . . . " According to the sixteenth chapter of St. Matthew's gospel, Jesus responded:

"I say . . . unto thee, that thou art Peter, and upon this rock I will build my church; and the gates of hell shall not prevail against it. And I will give unto thee the keys of the kingdom of heaven; and whatsoever thou shalt bind on earth shall be bound in heaven; and whatsoever thou shalt loose on earth shall be loosed in heaven."

Catholic scholars point out that the name Peter means "rock" in the Aramaic language which Jesus and his disciples spoke. Thus, they say, it is obvious that Jesus was speaking of Peter as the rock upon which he would build the church.

Some Protestant scholars contend that the "rock" to

which Jesus referred was not Peter himself, but his confession of faith in Jesus as the Saving One sent from God. This, they say, is the real foundation stone of the Church.

Other Protestants acknowledge that the Catholic reading of the text is the more plausible one. They go further and agree that Peter became, in actual fact, the principal leader of the early Christian community. *But*—and it is a formidable *but* indeed—they see no warrant in Scripture or the early history of the Church for exaggerating Peter's primacy of honor to the point of calling him "Prince" of the Apostles. On the contrary, they say, the Book of Acts and other New Testament evidence clearly indicate that Peter was regarded in his own lifetime merely as "first among equals" in the apostolic band.

Finally, they say, even if Peter did go to Rome and become its first bishop,* there is not sufficient reason for assuming that his special authority passed down, as a divinely guaranteed inheritance, to every subsequent Bishop of Rome. Supposing for the sake of argument that Apostolic authority did "descend" to the successors of the Apostles and that Peter had a special authority, would it not be more logical to say that Peter's authority passed to his successor as Bishop of Jerusalem—which was unquestionably the real center of the Christian world in his day— rather than to the man who followed him as Bishop of Rome, a job which he may have held late in his life, but

* The Bible does not mention a visit by Peter to Rome, and some Protestants doubt that he ever got there. But recent archaeological explorations under the high altar of St. Peter's Basilica have persuaded many objective observers that Peter was buried in Rome, at the site of the church which now bears his name, after dying a martyr's death in the reign of Emperor Nero.

which is not mentioned in the New Testament account of his career?

Aside from the whole question of "Petrine succession," many Protestants boggle at the idea of attributing infallibility to *any* human being or institution. They say that Catholicism comes close to idolatry (which is defined theologically as the worship of anything short of God) when it equates the voice of the Church with the voice of God. The Bible clearly teaches that God chooses to speak to men through ordinary, human (and hence fallible) channels. Even in the supreme act of revelation—the Incarnation—God accepted the limitations of human fallibility: Jesus was a *real* man, not a theophany. No Protestant would question that the guidance of the Holy Spirit is always available—and always right. But every Protestant would add that the Holy Spirit is not always heard and heeded in the Church—not even by popes.*

Finally, Protestants object strenuously to some of the conclusions that Catholics have drawn directly from their doctrine of authority.

The conclusion that most irritates Protestants and most seriously bedevils all moves toward Christian unity is that there can be only one true Church. (The idea of two or more infallible, divinely instituted organizations competing with one another for the world's attention is patently absurd.) And that "one true Church" must, of course, be the one headed by the successor to St. Peter. This doctrine

---

* In fairness to Catholic teaching, it should be pointed out that popes are presumed to be infallible only when they solemnly define issues of faith and morals for the guidance of the whole Church. Catholics readily acknowledge that popes can be wrong about such things as politics and the weather.

has been soft-pedaled considerably since the late Pope John XXIII set the Catholic Church on an ecumenical course. Protestants are no longer called "heretics"; they are "separated brethren."

The Second Vatican Council in its declaration on ecumenism went so far as to acknowledge that Protestants are in some sense related to the true Church through Christian baptism. But it quickly added that no one can be a full member of the true Church, and assured of access to all the means of grace, unless he is obedient to the authority of Rome.

Can the Church Err?

Another conclusion that Catholics have drawn from their doctrine of authority—in the past, at least—is that the Church can never fall into error sufficiently to need a real housecleaning. As one scholar has put it, Catholics can admit the need for reforms *in* the Church, but they consider it almost blasphemous to speak of a basic reform *of* the Church.

The Reverend Dr. Robert McAfee Brown, professor of religion at Stanford University, suggests in his excellent book *The Spirit of Protestantism* that "this is perhaps the ultimate issue dividing Protestantism and Roman Catholicism." He says that Protestantism, born in a great attempt at reformation of medieval Catholicism, has always taken very seriously the biblical injunction that judgment must "begin with the household of God."

"Protestantism affirms that the Church must be shaken, judged, purged and re-made," says Dr. Brown. "It cannot be renewed once. Its life must be a life of constant renewal, for it is 'a church of sinners,' a church that is constantly failing to fulfill its high calling. The attitude that must characterize the Church is the attitude of *repentance.*"

Most Protestants can pronounce a hearty amen to that sentiment. Most Catholics would be as horrified by it as they would be by an allegation that Jesus sometimes did wicked things. The reverence that a Catholic has for his Church is very similar to his reverence for Christ. A Protestant, on the other hand, instinctively regards all ecclesiastical institutions with suspicion if not scorn. His allegiance is directly and personally to Christ.

The Authority of Scripture

But how does the Protestant know what Christ is like, what he has taught, commanded, and promised? What is the Protestant's authority for holding any particular belief?

The Reformers' answer was "*sola scriptura*": the Bible is the sole and sufficient authority for all Christian doctrine. "Holy Scripture containeth all things necessary to salvation: so that whatsoever is not read therein, nor may be proved thereby, is not to be required of any man that it should be believed as an article of faith." So says the sixth of the famed Thirty-nine Articles of Religion that comprised the Reformation charter of the Church of England.

There is a widespread and entirely erroneous idea among Protestants that Catholics attach very little importance to the Bible, and indeed seldom read it. Actually, Catholic theology accords a very high and prominent place to Scripture. There are, however, two important differences between Catholic and Protestant attitudes toward the Bible. Whereas Protestants insist on the Bible as the *sole* source of doctrine, Catholics believe that *traditions* which have been handed down in the Church for centuries may also be considered vehicles of divine revelation. They point out that the Bible itself was the fruit of oral traditions that were circulated in the Church for many years before they were written down, and that the New Testament expressly says that there were "other things" that Jesus said and did which were not included in the Gospel accounts.

Who Interprets Scripture?

The second and even more profound difference is that Catholics are required as a basic point of obedience to accept any particular passage of Scripture in the sense in which it has been interpreted by the "infallible" teaching authority of the Church. Protestants have no such authoritative guide to the interpretation of scriptural passages which may be obscure or confusing. The Reformers dodged the whole question by insisting that the Bible "interprets itself"—that is, what is obscure in one passage may be clarified by a diligent search of other portions of Scripture. In practice, this turned out to mean that every man was his own ultimate authority on the Bible. If he wished to read it a certain way, no one had any power to contradict him, even though every scholar in Christendom might disagree with his exegesis. This is the so-called "principle of private interpretation" and it has had a very far-reaching impact on the development of Protestantism.

On one hand, it has served as the final guarantee of freedom of conscience among Protestants. From it has grown the Protestant emphasis on the right—and inescapable responsibility—of each human being to think through his own beliefs, and to make his own decision for (or against) Christ.

On the other hand, it has led to the fragmentation of Protestantism into more than two hundred denominations and sects. Ever since the Reformation, Protestant churches have been splitting apart, often with much bitterness on both sides, because of disagreements over interpretation of the Bible. And sometimes they have been very picayune disagreements indeed. Although the ecumenical movement in recent years has succeeded in patching up some long-standing divisions in the Protestant family, there are still, as we shall see in the next chapter, vast and strongly held differences, most of which are directly related to divergent interpretations of Scripture. It is not hard to see why Catholics refer to the Protestant principle of private interpretation as a charter for "theological anarchy."

The Adoration of Mary

How the Catholic Church has used tradition as a source of teachings which cannot be found in Scripture is illustrated by the cult of the Virgin Mary—the aspect of Catholicism which many Protestants find most repugnant.

The New Testament says relatively little about Mary. But what it does say is tremendously important. As the mother of Jesus, she was the human vehicle of the miracle of the Incarnation. And Scripture records that she undertook this awesome role in a spirit of humble obedience—

"be it unto me even as thou hast said." As her son was growing up, Mary was sometimes baffled by his conduct: St. Luke's gospel tells a touching story—almost certainly one of Mary's own reminiscences—of an occasion when the twelve-year-old Jesus disappeared during the family's annual Passover visit to Jerusalem, and was found later in the Temple, holding scholarly discourse with the teachers and wise men, who were "astonished at his understanding."

The Gospels record that Mary remained devoted to her son, following him after he set forth on his itinerant ministry and trying to look after his physical needs, which he was apt to neglect. She stood at the foot of his cross when he was crucified, and every parent must wonder in his heart who suffered the most terrible agony, Jesus or his mother.

This biblical account of Mary's role in the saving events centered around the life of Christ is sufficient to establish her right to the one honor which she had foreseen: "all generations shall call me blessed."

But the Catholic Church has not thought it right to stop there. On the basis of tradition, rather than Scripture, it has asserted that Mary herself was "immaculate" (sinless) from the moment of her conception in her mother's womb; and that upon her death she did not suffer corruption of the flesh but was "assumed" body and soul into heaven. And it has not made these added beliefs about Mary a matter of choice: they have been proclaimed as infallible dogmas, which every Catholic must believe in order to be saved.

The Church has also bestowed a host of new titles and

honors on Mary: "Mother of God," "Queen of Heaven," "Mediatrix of all Graces." It has encouraged the faithful to pray to Mary, and has stimulated the growth of "Marian devotions" to the point where in some areas they have become the center of Catholic worship. Catholic theologians insist that the Church does not permit "worship" of Mary, but only accords her "the highest veneration." They also say that Mary does not answer prayers in her own right, but "intercedes" with her son to obtain help for the faithful who pray to her. But it is at least open to question whether these distinctions are understood by all the Catholics who light candles at the foot of Mary's statue and participate in novenas to "our Lady."

A New Catholic Viewpoint

For a time, Catholic theology seemed to be moving headlong toward proclaiming Mary "Co-redemptrix" with Christ. This title, already widely used among Catholic bishops with no rebuke from the Vatican's Holy Office, makes Protestant blood run cold. It vividly demonstrates the basic Protestant objection to Catholic Mariology, namely, its tendency to obscure the distinctive role of Christ as the "only mediator between God and man."

Protestant fears were eased, if not removed, when the Second Vatican Council decided, by the paper-thin margin of 30 votes out of more than 2000, to forego a special schema, or Council declaration, on Mary, and to give her instead a chapter in the schema on the Church.

The importance of this widely misunderstood decision

is that it was a triumph for a relatively new viewpoint toward Mary which has been gaining strength in progressive Catholic circles. According to this viewpoint, which has been most influentially expounded by Pope Paul VI, Mary is to be thought of as "the model, the image, the ideal figure of the Church." In her humble, self-effacing obedience and complete trust, she is the prototype of what all members of the Church should be like. And in her willing cooperation with the work of redemption which God accomplished in Christ, she exemplifies the Church's mission on earth.

Protestant theologians find this new viewpoint on Mary infinitely more attractive than some of the other Mariological doctrines that have found credence in the Catholic Church.

If Protestants feel that Catholics give Mary too much honor, Catholics feel, with at least equal emotion, that Protestants give her far too little. Mary is seldom mentioned in the average Protestant church except at Christmas time.

A growing number of Protestant scholars acknowledge the justice of this indictment, and are urging Protestants to give Mary the reverence that is clearly—and biblically —her due.

"Not as a semi-divine being, but as an outstanding member of the communion of saints, she is blessed among women," says Jaroslav Pelikan. "When Protestants begin to say this out loud in their teaching and worship . . . they will be better prepared to speak a word of fraternal warning to their Roman Catholic brethren."

Saints, Purgatory, and Merit

There are other Catholic doctrines for which Protestants can find no warrant in Scripture. Catholics pray to a multitude of officially designated saints, in addition to Mary, in the belief that saints have the power to intercede in heaven on behalf of those who seek their help. Catholics also believe that each human soul is judged at the time of death, and, depending upon the presence or absence of "sanctifying grace," is consigned directly to heaven (the saints), irrevocably to hell (the damned), or temporarily to purgatory (the in-between fellow who is neither good enough to go straight to heaven, nor bad enough to be eternally condemned). In purgatory, according to Catholic theology, souls undergo "temporal punishment" to cleanse them of sin and prepare them for the perfect holiness of heaven. Christians on earth ("the Church Militant") can invoke the assistance of the saints in heaven ("the Church Triumphant") in procuring the release of souls from purgatory. In effect, the accounts of the souls in purgatory are balanced by placing to their credit some of the virtues which the saints have on deposit in heaven's "treasury of merits."

The whole idea of a "treasury of merits" is vaguely but distinctly offensive to many Protestants. It seems excessively legalistic, and leaves the impression that God's saving love is poured forth, not in gracious abundance, but according to a nicely calculated, almost mechanical formula. As for purgatory and the veneration of saints, the abiding verdict of Protestantism is expressed in the Thirty-nine Articles: both doctrines are "vainly invented, and grounded upon no warranty of Scripture, but rather repugnant to the Word of God."

Two Sacraments or Seven?

Although this catalogue of basic differences between Catholics and Protestants is already woefully long, we cannot terminate it without some reference to divergent views of the sacraments. By sacrament, both Catholics and Protestants mean an outward sign, or action, instituted by Christ as a channel through which divine help, or grace, is imparted.

Protestants recognize two sacraments: (1) *Baptism*, through which a human spirit is cleansed of "original sin" (understood as man's natural predilection to be self-centered, willful and disobedient to God) and endowed with a new kind of life; and (2) *Holy Communion* (also known as the Eucharist or the Lord's Supper), by which the baptized Christian is sustained and strengthened, and through which he is drawn into a closer fellowship with God and his fellow man.

Catholics recognize five other sacraments: confirmation, penance, extreme unction, holy orders, and matrimony. Their counterparts can be found in many Reformation churches: the principal point at issue is whether they are distinctively Christian sacraments on a par with baptism and the Eucharist.

Baptism

It may strike the reader as remarkable, after so much stress on differences, to learn that Catholics and Protestants have very similar ideas about baptism. Both affirm that it is primarily *God's action*, not man's. Some Protestants insist on the necessity for a response in faith by the person being baptized; they therefore practice only adult or "believer's baptism." But the vast majority of Protestants agree with the Catholic Church that infants can and should be baptized, because the efficacy of the action is altogether independent of the attitude of the recipient, or the credentials of the one who performs it. (The Catholic Church recognizes the validity of a baptism performed by a Protestant, or even one performed by an atheist, provided water is used and the name of the Trinity is properly invoked according to the biblical prescription.)

The Lord's Supper

When we come to the Eucharist, we find Catholics and Protestants agreeing that it was instituted by Jesus at his last supper with his disciples. According to the oldest existing account of the event, that found in St. Paul's first letter to the Church at Corinth, Jesus "took bread; and when he had given thanks, he broke it, and said, This is my body which is broken for you: do this in remembrance of me." After supper, "in like manner, he took the cup, saying, This cup is the new covenant in my blood:

do this as often as you shall drink it, in remembrance of me."

Some Protestants hold that Christians merely perform a "memorial" rite when they celebrate the Lord's Supper. But this is a distinctly minority view in the Christian family. Most Protestants believe that the Eucharist is a "re-presentation" of Christ's sacrifice on Calvary, and that Christ is "really present" in a mystical and incorporeal sense—every time it is celebrated.

Catholics go much further. To them the sacrifice of the Mass is a "renewal," or repetition, of the sacrifice on Calvary. The consecrated bread and wine do not merely symbolize the body and blood of Christ: they *are* the body and blood of Christ, in a literal sense. They retain the external appearance of bread and wine, but their true *substance* has been transformed on the altar (hence the term "transubstantiation," which is applied to this Catholic doctrine).

Protestants contend that the Catholic doctrine vitiates the "once-and-for-allness" of Christ's redemptive act, and that the emphasis on Christ's being literally and corporeally present on the altar tends to degrade a holy mystery into some kind of magic. They are particularly repelled by the cult of "tabernacle worship" that has grown up around the Catholic practice of "reserving" some of the consecrated bread on the altar, to be adored by the faithful as a visible presence of God.

Conversely, Catholics feel that Protestants have rationalized all the mystery out of the Eucharist. They point out that Jesus did *not* say, "This represents my body . . ."; he said, "This *is* my body."

No meeting of minds seems likely on this point in the foreseeable future. But in other aspects of their corporate worship, Catholics and Protestants are unmistakably moving closer together.

The Changing Forms of Worship

The Liturgical Constitution adopted by the Second Vatican Council permits most of the Mass, and all of the sacraments to be conducted in the language of the people rather than in Latin. It also calls for more emphasis on what Protestants call "the ministry of the Word," with a sermon now made a required part of every Sunday Mass. These and other reforms in Roman Catholic liturgy are aimed at making the laity active participants rather than passive spectators in worship.

Meanwhile, far-reaching changes are taking place in the worship of Protestant churches. Even in Baptist and Methodist churches, traditionally known for their informality, there is a marked trend toward vestments for the minister, robes for the choir, processionals to the chancel, formal rather than extemporaneous prayers. Most significant of all, the Lord's Supper is being celebrated more frequently, and as a full service in its own right rather than being tacked on to the regular preaching service once in a great while as a sort of afterthought.

We have by no means exhausted the list of Catholic-Protestant differences. Nothing has been said, for example, about "the priesthood of all believers" which the Reformers made such a fuss about and which all modern Protestants cherish, even though not one in ten has the least

notion what it's all about. Nor have we gone into such
things as confessing to a priest, or divorce, or birth control.
But perhaps we have covered enough of the really basic
differences to give you an idea why no one who is working
for Christian reunion expects to see it accomplished day
after tomorrow. "At this point, it seems humanly impos-
sible to resolve the profound differences which separate
Protestants and Catholics," says the Reverend Dr. William
J. Wolf, an Episcopal Church observer at the Vatican
Council. "But we have our Lord's personal assurance that
'with God, all things are possible.' If we can learn to live
together as brothers in a spirit of love rather than mutual
antagonism, if we work patiently at trying to understand
one another, and if we give the other fellow credit for being
just as sincere and devoted to Christ as we claim to be
—God in His own good time will show us the road to
unity."

CHAPTER IV

Is the Bible Infallible?

There is far more diversity in the Roman Catholic Church than the average Protestant realizes. Catholics not only are free to disagree on politics, economics, international affairs, art, literature, music, and whether a steak should be cooked rare or medium; they also differ on a number of religious questions, as the lively debates at the Second Vatican Council have demonstrated.

But on central doctrines of the faith—such as the Incarnation—Catholics *are* united. Their unity is the result of obedience rather than consensus. When the Church declares a doctrine to be based on revealed truth, all Catholics must accept it on pain of mortal sin, whether or not they have previously found the evidence persuasive. They accept it because they believe that the Church is divinely endowed with infallible teaching authority—that God will not allow it to err on really vital points of faith (see pp. 49ff.).

To Protestants, this is the great scandal of Catholicism: people are "told what to believe."

To Catholics, the great scandal of Protestantism is that people are *not* "told what to believe."

When Protestants disagree on a point of doctrine, there is no final arbiter to say who is right. The sixteenth-century Reformers expected the Bible to take the place of the Pope as the ultimate yardstick of doctrine. But history has abundantly demonstrated that sincere men can draw quite different meanings from the Bible. Once Protestants had embraced the principle of private interpretation (p. 52), there was nothing to prevent them from drifting into widely divergent views on basic theological questions—including the authority of the Bible itself.

When Luther and Calvin Disagreed

This danger became evident fairly early in the Reformation. Martin Luther accepted it as a price that had to be paid for the kind of religious freedom that can lead to genuine personal commitment as opposed to mere assent. But John Calvin tried to forestall the problem by attributing to the Bible the same kind of infallibility that Roman Catholics attribute to the Church. Although Luther protested this creation of a "paper pope," Calvin's view gradually prevailed. By the seventeenth century, most of Protestantism was committed to Calvin's dictum that believers should accord to Scripture "the same complete credit and authority . . . as if they had heard the very words pronounced by God Himself."

Belief in the "verbal inerrancy" of the Bible is based on logic very similar to that which Catholics use in defending the concept of papal infallibility. God could not take a chance on men misunderstanding the self-revelation which He accomplished through the history of Israel, and supremely in the life, death, and resurrection of Jesus Christ. Therefore He inspired the writers of the Bible to set down a wholly accurate, completely dependable record. His "superintendency" of the writing of the Bible extended to the very choice of words. Thus the Bible must be revered as "the Word of God" in a quite literal sense.

During the eighteenth and nineteenth centuries, the doctrine of verbal inerrancy was brought sharply into question. The scientific knowledge which man was beginning to acquire flatly contradicted some of the things stated in the Bible—for example, the assertion in the first chapter of Genesis that only six days elapsed between the creation of the cosmos and the emergence of human life on this planet. These contradictions would not have bothered Luther, who never regarded all parts of the Bible as being of equal value, and who held that the primary importance of Scripture was its witness to Jesus Christ. But the admission of the slightest error in the Bible was intolerable to Protestants who had staked their faith on the proposition that every word in the Old and New Testaments was virtually dictated by God.

The Birth of Liberalism

This crisis led to a theological revolution in Protestantism, and the emergence of a school of thought known as *Liberalism*. It began, as do most new fashions in theology, in German universities. By the latter part of the nineteenth century it had spread widely through Europe, Great Britain, and America.

The theological high priests of Liberalism were such German professors as Friedrich Schleiermacher, Albrecht Ritschl, Adolf von Harnack, and Rudolf Bultmann. In the United States, its notable proponents included Harry Emerson Fosdick, A. N. Wieman, and Rufus Jones.

Although these men differed on many points, they shared a common concern for making Christianity palatable to modern minds. In Dr. Fosdick's words, they sought to differentiate between the "abiding essence" of the Christian message, and the myths, legends, and stories used to convey that message in the Bible.

The Liberals did not merely abandon the idea that the Bible was infallible. Many of them went further and refused to accord any special authority to the Scriptures. They increasingly came to look upon the Bible simply as an ancient book which might, if subjected to proper critical study, yield some reliable data about the life of Jesus and the history of Israel. This attitude was reflected in the vogue of "higher criticism" which swept through German theological schools in the nineteenth century.

In their attempt to reduce Christianity to its "essentials," Liberals proceeded on the a priori assumption that God always acts through "natural" forces and there is no such thing as a "supernatural" event. Thus Liberalism sought to find natural explanations for the miracles recorded in the New Testament, from the feeding of the five thousand to the Resurrection. What it could not explain away, it soft-pedaled, or labeled "myth."

The most radical expressions of Liberalism jettisoned

the concept of a personal God in favor of what Professor Daniel B. Stevick has aptly described as "the worship of abstractions spelled with capital letters." God became an Immanent Principle of the natural universe, which worked toward goodness. Jesus was "the most admirable embodiment so far of this divine principle," a Way-shower whose example all men should emulate. But he was just an humble, human teacher, trying to preach a simple message about the fatherhood of God and the brotherhood of man, and he doubtless would have been appalled at the thought that his followers would some day be calling him the Son of God.

The less extreme liberals, including such leaders as Fosdick and Jones, continued to believe in a God who transcends the order of nature (as well as works through it) and to insist on the uniqueness of Jesus. Some of these "moderate" liberals were prepared to look upon Jesus as the Incarnate Self-Expression of God. But many others were inclined to the view that Jesus is supreme and unique only in that he fulfilled more completely than any other person ever has the potentiality of every human being to become a child of God.

The Social Gospel

The left wing of Liberalism shaded off imperceptibly into humanism (pp. 8ff.), and the whole movement was infected with a strong faith in the perfectibility of man and his society. This led to Liberalism's greatest constructive achievement: its powerful emphasis on the "social gospel," which commits Christians to work here and now for the elimination of injustice and the bettering of human living standards. If Protestant Christianity today is at long last taking an effective part in the struggle for Negro rights, and an intelligent interest in the maintenance of peace, Liberalism is largely responsible. However skeptical they may be about some of the other things Jesus is reported to have said and done, Liberals have always taken very seriously the words attributed to him in the twenty-fifth chapter of Matthew: "Inasmuch as you have done it [kind deeds] to the least of these my brothers, you have done it [them] unto me."

But Liberalism's faith that man could be saved from sin by education and from travail by science proved to be its Achilles' heel. The rise of Adolf Hitler and the murder of 6 million Jews in the very country that gave birth to Liberal theology; the terrible slaughter which the most highly educated nations inflicted upon one another in World War II; and the realization that science had opened the door to total annihilation by nuclear weapons—these and other events of recent history have made even the most dedicated Liberal wonder whether there may not be something after all in the classic Christian view that man is helpless to save himself, that he is rather dependent on the mercy of God to extricate him from his human predicament.

Fundamentalism

Liberalism was one Protestant response to the challenge of modern science. There was another response, exactly opposite to Liberalism and bitterly hostile toward it. This second response came to be known as *Fundamentalism*. It developed in the United States in the early part of the twentieth century. Its great theologian was J. Gresham Machen. Its popular lay leader was William Jennings Bryan (who defended the Fundamentalist cause against the slashing ridicule of atheist attorney Clarence Darrow in the famous Scopes evolution trial at Dayton, Tennessee, in 1925).

Fundamentalism got its name from a series of pamphlets published between 1909 and 1915 under the title *The Fundamentals: A Testimony to Truth*. Written by various conservative Protestant scholars, these theological essays upheld the following as "fundamental" Christian doctrines: belief in the inerrancy of the Bible; the virgin birth; the physical resurrection of Jesus; a "substitutionary" theory of the atonement (that is, one which holds that Jesus died in man's stead, satisfying the requirements of Divine justice through vicarious suffering for the sins of the whole world); and the expectation of a physical "Second Coming" of Christ, when he will judge the world.

These doctrines were singled out for defense not because they sum up the Christian faith (after all, the linchpin doctrine of the Incarnation is included only by inference), but because they were under attack by liberal theologians bent on stripping away all "supernatural" elements from Christianity. Fundamentalism can be understood only as a strong emotional reaction against the reductionism of Liberal theology.

The cornerstone of Fundamentalism from the start was an uncompromising insistence on the "verbal inerrancy" of all parts of the Bible. This often-used phrase meant that the Bible was totally without error, and that its very language, as well as its general content, was directly inspired by God. "To the Fundamentalist, this doctrine became the first defense against error," says Professor William Hordern. "If one began by doubting any statement of the Bible, he had started down the slippery slope that, the Fundamentalist believed, would lead to the denial of God and the divinity of Jesus, the loss of certainty of salvation, and finally the loss of ethics."

In fairness to the Fundamentalist position, which is more often caricatured than explained, it should be pointed out that belief in the Bible's infallibility is not the same thing as "taking the Bible literally." The Fundamentalist recognizes that there is poetic and allegorical language in the Bible, and that Jesus himself often used vivid figures of speech, such as his advice to cut off an offending hand, which he meant to be understood in spiritual rather than literal terms. What the Fundamentalist tries to do is to follow the "natural" meaning of each scriptural passage. When the Bible claims to be recording factual history—as it unquestionably does, for example, in the accounts of the Resurrection—the Fundamentalist takes it as literally "God's truth."

Salvation and Piety

Whereas Liberalism was concerned with the social implications of the Christian gospel, Fundamentalism focused its attention on individual salvation and personal piety. It was not indifferent to the ills of society, but it held that the best way to deal with them was to "change the hearts of men." It also was much preoccupied with the end of the world and the traumatic sequence of "last things" that would accompany the return of Christ as Judge. Its ethical concerns reflected a distrust of modern life, and were expressed in prohibitions on dancing, card-playing, Sunday movies, and the use of alcoholic beverages and tobacco.

Fundamentalism had great appeal for Protestants who found Liberalism's gospel a very thin soup, and who were looking for the same kind of religious "certainties" which the Roman Catholic Church promises to its adherents. During the 1920s and 1930s, Liberalism and Fundamentalism waged a titanic struggle for control of Protestant denominations in America. When the smoke of battle cleared, the Liberals had apparently won in most of the major communions. But Fundamentalists were clearly dominant in two large denominations—the Southern Baptist Convention and the Lutheran Church–Missouri Synod. They also held sway in scores of smaller denominations (including some which split off from the major Methodist and Presbyterian bodies during the struggle). And there were Fundamentalist minorities of various sizes in other Protestant communions.

Modern Orthodoxy

By the mid-1930s, Liberalism had a firm grip on the seminaries and other seats of institutional power of the major Protestant denominations. But its dominance proved to be short-lived. Within a very few years, it was in headlong retreat before a new theology to which various labels have been applied, but which is probably best described in the term *Modern Orthodoxy*. Among the theologians who have played formative roles in the emergence of Modern Orthodoxy are Karl Barth and Emil Brunner in Europe; William Temple and C. S. Lewis in England; John and D. M. Baillie in Scotland; Reinhold Niebuhr and John C. Bennett in the United States.

Professor William Hordern gives an excellent capsule summary of Modern Orthodoxy in his book *A Layman's Guide to Protestant Theology* (which is warmly recommended to any reader who would like to delve more deeply into the questions discussed in this chapter):

"The heart of this movement lies in loyalty to the faith of historic orthodoxy, not because it is ancient or orthodox, but because it is believed to be true. Modern Orthodoxy believes that in the orthodox Christian tradition we have a precious heritage of truth which must not be thrown overboard just because someone has split the atom and someone else has looked farther through a telescope. Nevertheless, it is willing to understand the old truth more fully insofar as modern thought makes that possible."

Modern Orthodoxy rejects the Fundamentalist doctrine of "verbal inerrancy" as an aberration that crept into Protestant theology during the post-Reformation quest for an authority to take the place of the Pope. Instead of pinning its faith on an infallible book, it focuses on Christ as the only completely trustworthy source of knowledge about God. To treat the words of the Bible as the words of God is to erect an idol. It is to Christ the Revealer that men must look if they wish to encounter the Living God and hear His authentic Word to mankind.

"The Bible as a book is not the revelation," says John C. Bennett. "Every part of the Bible must be subjected to rigorous criticism and understood on its human side as the work of fallible men whose minds reflected the limitations of outlook of a particular time and culture. No event or teaching is to be guaranteed as authentic merely because it is in the Bible.

"On the other hand, the Bible *is* the record of the revelatory events in which God has made Himself known to man. It also contains the earliest record of the response of the Apostles and the earliest Christian community to these revelatory events—to Christ, his teaching, his death and the events associated with his resurrection."

Karl Barth goes further. While he welcomes the most radical scrutiny of biblical texts, he reminds theologians that—once they have satisfied themselves what the biblical authors really meant to convey—they have no right to substitute their own judgment for what the firsthand witnesses say they saw and heard.

"The post-biblical theologian may, no doubt, possess a better astronomy, geography, sociology, psychology, physiology, and so on than these biblical witnesses possessed," says the great Swiss theologian. "But he is not justified in comporting himself in relationship to those witnesses as though he knew more about the Word of God than they. . . . Even the smallest, strangest, simplest, or obscurest among the biblical witnesses has an incomparable advantage over even the most pious, scholarly, and sagacious latter-day theologian. From his special point of view, the witness has written about the revelatory act in direct confrontation with it." In other words, he was there.

While recoiling on one hand from the "bibliolatry" of Fundamentalism, Modern Orthodoxy is equally emphatic in rejecting Liberalism's attempt to reduce the Christian gospel to a few simple ethical teachings. From Reinhold Niebuhr and others, it has learned that the great biblical themes of sin, grace, and redemption are as relevant to modern man as they were to his forefathers. Modern Orthodoxy has not settled on any one doctrine of atonement. But it takes very seriously the basic biblical affirmation that "God was in Christ, reconciling the world unto Himself." In the words of Professor Hordern, it looks upon the Resurrection as "not simply an announcement that there is a life hereafter" but "a decisive turning point for the human race," a mighty act at the juncture of time and eternity through which God "proclaims the fact that there is a power at work in the world which is mightier than all the forces that crucified our Lord."

Modern Orthodoxy has retained Liberalism's passion for social justice, while learning to be far more realistic about the obstacles that human nature places in the way of its achievement. It is characteristic of Modern Orthodoxy to denounce segregation as a sin and to preach human brotherhood as a Christian ideal, while lobbying effectively for passage of a strong federal civil rights law to curb overt acts of discrimination by persons who don't really care about God's will in regard to race relations.

Another distinctive feature of Modern Orthodoxy is its rediscovery of the Church, not as a convenient institution for propagating Christian beliefs, but as the mystical Body of Christ. The inevitable result of taking the Church more seriously has been concern about its disunity, and it is no coincidence that the ecumenical movement has received its greatest impetus from the main-line Protestant denominations, in which Modern Orthodoxy has most thoroughly displaced Liberalism and Fundamentalism.

The Radical Reinterpreters

Although it casts a much smaller shadow than it did in the first half of this century, Liberalism is still a live option in Protestantism, and it has lately showed some evidences of new vitality. Thirty years after it ceased to be a burning issue in Europe, Rudolf Bultmann's "demythologizing" approach to the Bible has become a burning topic of conversation among American seminarians. A few theologians, such as Schubert M. Ogden, Paul van Buren, and William Hamilton, have written books expounding a Neo-liberal belief that traditional Christian doctrines must be "radically reinterpreted" (by which they usually mean abandoned) in order to sell the faith to modern intellectuals.

In 1963 Anglican Bishop John A. T. Robinson stirred up several old themes of German liberalism and marketed them to a mass audience in a book entitled *Honest to God*, which was so muddled in its theological concepts that Professor Alasdair McIntyre felt constrained to welcome the Bishop into the ranks of atheism. Dr. Robinson hastily rejected the welcome. He said he was only trying to make God "real and relevant and urgent for our generation" by separating the essential Christian message from "the envelope in which the message was sent." That, of course, is precisely what Bultmann said he was trying to do: separate the "kernel" of Christian truth from the "husk of a pre-scientific world view."

The trouble with this effort, as Karl Barth has repeatedly pointed out, is that each theologian brings to the biblical message his own presuppositions about what constitutes "kernel" and what may be discarded as "husk." The net effect of most recent Neo-liberal attempts to rewrite the Gospel has been to scrap all its supernatural elements, on the unproved (and unprovable) premise that they are "husk," and to translate what is left into the terminology of existential philosophy. Thus, sin becomes "alienation," salvation becomes "realizing the potential of authentic existence," and the Resurrection becomes a "symbol" of the early Christian community's faith that this is a pretty good world after all.

So far, Neo-liberalism seems to have nothing to say that was not said earlier—and on the whole, better—by Liberalism.

The Evangelicals

Meanwhile, Fundamentalism still holds the strongholds it won during the twenties. Because of their strong emphasis on evangelism, Fundamentalist denominations have grown more rapidly than main-line Protestant bodies, and Fundamentalism today encompasses a substantial portion—perhaps a third—of the total membership of Protestant churches in the United States. It is much weaker in Western Europe, where it never won a very wide foothold, but is thriving in Latin America as a result of vigorous missionary efforts.

In recent years, it has showed signs of mellowing, of becoming slightly less embattled and truculent in its attitude toward the "heretics" who do not share its beliefs. There also have been signs of a greater openness to intellectual inquiry, and a desire to communicate with the contemporary world in its own language—if not on the basis of its presuppositions.

Many of the modern heirs of the Fundamentalist movement prefer to be called "evangelicals," or "conservatives." They include such theologians as E. J. Carnell and Carl F. Henry, who can hold their own in scholarly disputation with anyone. Some of them—Carnell is one—are even willing to go along with a modified theory of evolution. But one and all stand firmly on the doctrine of verbal inerrancy. Regarding themselves as the only true "Bible-believing Christians," they tend to stand aloof from the ecumenical movement that is drawing other Protestants closer together, and to eschew any ties with such cooperative organizations as the National Council of Churches (which most Fundamentalists look upon as being heavily infiltrated with unrepentant Liberals or worse). About forty Fundamentalist bodies have banded together in the National Association of Evangelicals.

On the extreme right wing of Fundamentalism are the followers of radio preacher Carl McIntire and like-minded souls, who have formed the American Council of Christian Churches. They are so Fundamentalist that they regard Southern Baptists as dangerous liberals. Someone has suggested that they really should be given their own designation—perhaps "Separatists"—because of their insistence on avoiding any kind of fellowship with other Christians whose views on the infallibility of the Bible they regard as insufficiently rigorous.

CHAPTER V

The Protestant Faith Families:

The Great Reformation Churches

In a pleasant American suburb, a polite young lady of twelve went to call on the new family that had just moved into the house next door. She was delighted to find that it included a girl of approximately her own age. They were soon deeply involved in the kind of mutual cross-examination that always takes place under such circumstances. Finally, they got around to religion.

"We are Presbyterians," said the Welcoming Committee. "What are you?"

The newcomer hesitated, uncertain how to answer.

"Well," she said at last, "Papa is an Episcopalian, and Mamma is a Lutheran. I'm not sure what we kids are. We were Methodists in our last neighborhood, because the Methodist Church was nearby. Maybe I'll go to church with you."

She did that the next Sunday. Her report on the church's architecture, the pastor's personality, and the congregation's friendliness was so enthusiastic that her parents decided to follow her example. Before the packing crates had been cleared away, the whole family had become Presbyterian.

This kind of thing happens all the time. In religion as in everything else, ours is a mobile society. Individuals and families shift their allegiance from one Protestant denomination to another as casually as they switch brands of toothpaste. The traffic back and forth across denominational lines is so heavy that the lines are becoming blurred and indistinct. Today, if a pastor refers to "our denominational heritage," he can be reasonably sure that one fourth of the congregation won't know what he's talking about—and another fourth won't care.

As the previous chapter indicated, there are still serious theological differences among Protestants. But they are no longer primarily *denominational* differences. Instead, they cut across denominational lines. A fundamentalist Baptist is much closer in outlook and convictions to a fundamentalist Lutheran than he is to a liberal Baptist.

The steady erosion of once-sharp points of difference is both a result and a cause of the ecumenical movement, which has drawn main-line Protestant bodies into closer relationships in recent years. Ecumenical dialogue has cleared up many ancient misunderstandings, and brought to light many situations in which Protestants of different traditions were not really so far apart as they had thought on doctrinal matters. At the same time, the laity's plainly manifested impatience with denominationalism has provided a great stimulus to the quest for unity.

Although denominational loyalties have grown weaker

and denominational differences less important than they were in past generations, the Protestant who wants to belong to a community of faith still faces the inexorable necessity of choosing a denomination. Just as he cannot buy toothpaste without opting for one particular brand, so he cannot join a church without identifying himself with one particular denomination.*

This being the case, the more thoughtful church-joiners find themselves asking: What's the difference? What will I encounter in an Episcopal service of Morning Prayer that I would not find at a Quaker meeting? What does a Seventh-day Adventist believe that a Lutheran doesn't believe—and vice versa? Do Presbyterians run their churches the same way as do the Disciples of Christ?

As soon as you begin looking into such questions, you discover that while historical distinctions between Protestant denominations have become less vivid, they have by no means disappeared entirely. There are still differences— in ethos, doctrine, forms of worship, patterns of organization, and traditional attitudes. And these differences may be quite important to the person seeking a church home or trying to understand the one in which he finds himself.

The remainder of this chapter and the following two chapters will be devoted to thumbnail sketches of the principal denominational families of Protestantism, as well as to several movements that are related to Protestantism historically, although they can hardly be called Protestant in theology.

* There are some "nondenominational" churches that offer a bland mixture of several Protestant traditions. But in practice each such church tends to become a small denomination in its own right.

It will be easier to keep track of the relationships between Protestant bodies if we review them in roughly chronological order, beginning with the three great Reformation churches that emerged during the sixteenth century.

THE LUTHERANS

The oldest and still the largest Protestant denomination in the world is the one that bears Martin Luther's name.

Luther is one of the most fascinating figures in history —and one of the handful who can be legitimately credited with having altered its course.

He was born in the German state of Saxony in 1483, the same year as the Italian painter Raphael. Although he came of poor peasant stock, he had great drive and ambition. He worked his way through school (sometimes he was reduced to begging in the streets for food) and received a law degree from the University of Erfurt in 1505.

In that same year, Luther had some personal experience that turned his attention toward religion. What it was, he never said—it was one of the very few aspects of his private life about which he was reticent. But it was sufficient to cause him to abandon his career as a lawyer and become a monk in an Augustinian monastery.

The medieval Catholic Church into which Luther plunged was not a lovely institution. There were flagrant corruption and immorality among its clergy. It was commonplace for priests to live with concubines and to father illegitimate children. One Belgian bishop, famous for his promiscuity, boasted publicly that in the twenty-two months past he had sired fourteen bastards. The moral rot extended right up to the papacy. Several of the medieval popes were notorious rum-pots and womanizers; one of them, Alexander VI, was such an insatiable lecher that he had the ceiling of his bedroom in the Vatican decorated with pornographic paintings.

Many of the clergy were ignorant of such elemental aspects of the Christian faith as the Apostles' Creed and the Lord's Prayer. The "religion" they taught was a caricature of true Catholic theology, a compound of crude superstitions. But for all its shortcomings, the medieval Church possessed vast power.

"The Church invaded a man's life at every point, and the role of the priest was decisive," says Reformation historian William Stevenson. "Without the priest's mediation, salvation was unattainable. The unbaptized could not be saved, and only the Church could administer baptism; no sinner could be saved without confession and absolution, and only a lawfully ordained priest could hear confession and speak the word of peace. The Church kept a strangle hold upon the souls of men, with power to open or shut fast the gates of heaven."

But it was not the corruption of the Church that troubled Martin Luther during his first three years as a friar. He was totally preoccupied with a sense of his own sinfulness. He tried to ease his hair-shirt conscience by rigorous acts of penance. But no matter how much he starved and beat his body, no matter how many hours he spent kneeling on the stone floor of his monastery cell in prayer, he never felt that he had succeeded in bridging the gap between God's holiness and his own unworthiness.

The light dawned in Luther's life on the day when, as he searched the Bible, he found in St. Paul's Epistle to the Romans the assurance that men are saved by faith in God's mercy, rather than by their own strivings (see p. 44). The immediate effect of this discovery was to liberate Luther from his agonized absorption with his own salvation, enabling him to turn his attention to helping others. In 1508 he left the monastery and joined the faculty of the University of Wittenberg, where he quickly acquired a reputation as a brilliant scholar and powerful preacher.

Indulgences for Sale

It was at this point that Luther began to be painfully aware of the abuses that were rampant in the Church. For nine long years, he brooded about them, and became increasingly convinced that the Church had drifted very far from the teachings of the Bible. In 1517 he was finally goaded into public protest. Pope Leo X was trying to raise money for the enlargement and embellishment of St. Peter's Church in Rome. He sent official Vatican salesmen into various countries, including Germany, to peddle "indulgences." In theory, an indulgence was a papal pardon through which a penitent sinner could obtain remission of the temporal punishment which he would otherwise receive in purgatory. In theory also, the indulgences were not sold: they were bestowed in recognition of the act of contrition that the repentant sinner performed in making a donation to the Church. But in practice these

fine theological distinctions were lost. Ordinary people regarded indulgences as licenses to sin that could be bought
from the Church.

The indulgence salesman who worked Luther's territory
was a Dominican friar named John Tetzel. He was a
spiritual ancestor of the Madison Avenue pitchman, and
he did not complicate his hard sell with any theological
window dressing. He simply posted a price list for various
sins.

The outraged Luther wrote a blistering denunciation of
the sale of indulgences. Then he went on to list some of
the other things he found wrong with the Church. By the
time he had finished, he had set down ninety-five protests.
On All Saints' Eve in the year 1517, he nailed his "theses"
on the door of the church at Wittenberg.

A Spark in Dry Tinder

Looking back, it is possible to say that the Protestant Reformation began at that moment. But Luther certainly did
not realize that he was starting a vast historical movement
that would divide Christendom. He had no thought of
starting a new church; he simply wanted to reform the
Catholic Church.

But the spark he struck fell into dry tinder. "There was
the resentful feeling all over Germany that the nation was
being exploited by Rome and impoverished by burdensome exactions in order to maintain the splendor of the
papal court," says Stevenson, in *The Story of the Reformation.* "Luther's theses had an unprecedented circulation,

being read all over Germany within a few weeks, and Germany was solidly behind the Reformer."

Even so, it took three years for Luther to reach the point of an open break with Rome. Those three years were filled with dramatic confrontations between Luther and papal representatives, who tried in vain to get the stubborn monk to recant. Luther began by insisting that there is no need for human mediation between a man's soul and God; salvation is a free gift which men receive through the medium of faith. It cannot be doled out by the Church at will; nor can any priest or pope slam the door of heaven in the face of any man who puts his faith in Jesus Christ.

In defending this position, Luther was driven finally to deny the authority of the Pope, and to rest his whole case on the Bible as the only yardstick of Christian doctrine. He also denied that ordination conferred special powers on priests and bishops that laymen did not possess. Instead, he proclaimed the "priesthood of all believers."

His views, circulated widely through Europe in a series of pamphlets, attracted such a following that Pope Leo X resorted to his ultimate weapon—one which in years past had not failed to bring even kings and emperors to their knees. He excommunicated Luther. On December 10, 1520, Luther went to the courtyard of Wittenberg University and in the presence of a group of students publicly burned the papal bull of excommunication. It was an act of defiance comparable to Caesar's crossing of the Rubicon. The Lutheran Church came into being that night.

Under the powerful protection of German princes who were delighted to cast off Roman ecclesiastical authority, the mother church of Protestantism grew rapidly. When

Luther died, in 1546, it was firmly implanted in northern Germany and had spread into Denmark, Sweden, Norway, and Finland.

The Lutherans Today

Today there are about 75 million Lutherans in the world. They constitute almost one third of the world's total Protestant population. There are Lutheran churches on every continent, but Germany and Scandinavia remain the stronghold of Lutheranism, accounting for about 90 per cent of its world-wide membership.

The first Lutheran congregation in North America was established in 1638 by a group of Swedes who settled along the Delaware River. For the next century, there was comparatively little immigration from Northern Europe, so the Lutheran foothold in the new world grew very slowly. It was not until 1748 that Pastor Henry Melchior Muhlenberg, patriarch of American Lutheranism, was able to find enough scattered churches to organize the first synod.

During the nineteenth century, millions of German and Scandinavian immigrants flocked to America. With them they brought not only the Lutheran faith, but also the particular expression of it that they had known in the national churches of their homelands. "Hyphenated" Lutheran churches sprang up through Pennsylvania, Ohio, the Middle West, and the Mississippi Valley, where most of the northern European immigrants settled. There were German-Lutheran churches for the Germans, Swedish-Lutheran churches for the Swedes, Danish-Lutheran churches for the Danes, and so on. Most of them conducted services in the congregation's native European language rather than English. And each church had very little to do with Lutherans of a different nationality.

By the time the great waves of immigration ended early in the twentieth century, American Lutheran churches were deeply entrenched in a tradition that set them apart from each other and from the mainstream of American life.

But in the decades since World War II, American Lutherans have broken out of this mold. Vigorous evangelism has brought in millions of new members who have no trace of German or Scandinavian ancestry. The Lutherans now rank as the third largest Protestant group in the United States—behind the Baptists and Methodists. Meanwhile, a series of mergers have drastically reduced denominational fragmentation. Most of the 8 million Lutherans in this country now belong to three strong national bodies —the Lutheran Church in America, the American Lutheran Church, and the Lutheran Church–Missouri Synod. The first two are not far apart in doctrine and polity, and they may eventually merge. The Missouri Synod is fundamentalist in doctrine, and has remained aloof, not only from merger movements, but even from such cooperative Protestant organizations as the National Council of Churches.

Lutheran Worship

In fidelity to Luther's teachings, Lutheran churches observe two sacraments—baptism and Holy Communion. They baptize infants (as well as adult converts) in the conviction that baptism is an act in which God gives Himself to one who is absolutely helpless, who has no merits of his own to offer (not even the merit of personal faith), and who can only receive the free gift of grace. They believe that Christ is "really present" in the sacrament of Holy Communion, but reject the Catholic doctrine of transubstantiation which holds that the bread and wine become literally the body and blood of Christ at the moment of consecration.

Lutheran worship has retained many features of Catholic liturgy in a simplified form. Lutherans observe the seasons of the historic Church year; they use altars, crosses, candles, and vestments. Music is traditionally superb in Lutheran churches. Luther himself wrote several hymns, including the magnificent A Mighty Fortress Is Our God, and much of the world's greatest religious music was composed by a Lutheran, Johann Sebastian Bach.

Perhaps because they feel secure in their ancient liturgy, Lutherans are not afraid to house it in ultra-modern architecture. Many of the most striking contemporary American churches are Lutheran.

Some Lutheran churches in Europe have bishops. But all Lutheran bodies in the United States have what is known in church jargon as congregational polity. This means that the local congregation is the main focus of real authority, with certain powers delegated to regional synods or national conferences or conventions.

The new look in American Lutheranism is reflected in an increasing and skillful use of modern methods of mass communication. The motion picture Martin Luther, produced under church sponsorship, proved to be one of the biggest hits in years. The Lutheran Hour on radio consistently draws one of the largest audiences of any in the field of religious broadcasting. *The Lutheran*, a biweekly magazine, is regarded enviously by other Protestants as one of the finest denominational news publications in existence.

Lutherans have also been active in relieving the burdens of the poor. Through Lutheran World Relief, they have shipped millions of pounds of food and clothing to destitute families in other countries, and have helped to resettle and care for thousands of refugees.

Some Lutherans—mainly in the Missouri Synod—feel strongly about educating their children in a frankly Christian environment. As a result, Lutherans operate one of the nation's largest networks of parochial schools, second only to that of the Roman Catholic Church.

THE PRESBYTERIANS

On July 10, 1509—a few months after Luther began teaching at Wittenberg—John Calvin was born in the French town of Noyon. From early childhood, he displayed remarkable intellectual ability. At the age of fourteen, he was sent to Paris to study law. He made a brilliant record at the university, but discovered, as had Luther before him, that he was more interested in theology than in law. At the age of twenty-six, Calvin published the first edition of *The Institutes of the Christian Religion*, one of the most significant books in the history of the world. It outlined a comprehensive system of Protestant doctrine that was similar to Luther's teaching in many respects, but quite different in others.

By the time the *Institutes* appeared, Calvin had moved from his native France to Geneva, Switzerland. The book made him famous almost overnight. He was hailed as "the Aristotle of the Reformation," and for nearly thirty years he dominated both the civic and religious life of Geneva. People flocked to Geneva from all over Europe to sit at Calvin's feet and absorb his wisdom. By the time he died, in 1564, his theology had been adopted by Protestant churches in Switzerland, France, Holland, Hungary, and Scotland. Calvinist teachings even invaded Luther's Germany—much to Luther's exasperation.

What Calvin Taught

The distinctive theme of Calvin's theology was the absolute sovereignty of God. Calvin was never troubled by the question asked by so many of us in the face of great tragedies, "How could a loving God let this happen?" To Calvin, the answer was that God, having created the universe and all that is therein, was totally free to do with it as He pleased. God made the rules, so whatever He did must be just and right, however dimly its rightness might be perceived by a human creature of limited understanding and vision.

Complementing this emphasis on God's sovereignty was Calvin's assertion that man is totally guilty and depraved. He is helpless in his sins, and can do nothing to save himself. Although he does not deserve salvation, God in His mercy sent His Son, Jesus Christ, to redeem man from corruption. If men have faith in Christ, their sins are forgiven and the righteousness of Christ is imputed to them vicariously, so that they are made acceptable in God's sight. But not all men are to be saved. God has elected, or "predestined," some to be saved and others to be damned. This is what Calvin called the "double decree," and he admitted that he found it a horrible thought that God should have determined in advance that some poor creatures would be doomed to spend eternity in hell. But he felt that he was driven by the logic of his theological system to defend the concept of the double decree. "Predestination, by which God adopts some to the hope of life, and adjudges others to eternal death, no one, desirous of the credit of piety, dares absolutely to deny," he said. "For men are not all created with a similar destiny; but eternal life is foreordained for some, and eternal damnation for others."

Calvin's doctrine of predestination is a classic example of the difficulties a theologian can get himself into when he feels that he must follow a particular biblical teaching (in this case, the sovereignty of God) to what he considers its logical conclusion, without taking into account other teachings that are of equal importance.

To follow his idea as far as it would lead him, Calvin had to walk roughshod over the doctrine of free will, not to mention all that Christ taught about the love and mercy of our Father in heaven.

While few men had the nerve—or the intellectual prowess—to dispute with Calvin face to face, he was not long in his grave before his followers began to tone down his ideas about predestination. Jacob Arminius, a Dutch theologian, took the lead in modifying Calvinist theology to make room for free will and soft-pedal the notion that God foreordains any soul to damnation. Most Calvinist churches today are "Arminian" in their attitude toward predestination, and many have quietly swept the whole idea under the rug.

Lutheran-Calvinist Differences

One of the points on which Calvin differed from Luther —and one that proved fatal to an early attempt to unite their two branches of Protestantism—was the nature of the elements in Holy Communion. As noted earlier, Luther and his followers held that Christ is "really present" in the bread and wine, in a mystic and miraculous way, although not in the literal sense of the Catholic doctrine of transubstantiation. Calvin felt that Luther's view was much too close to transubstantiation, and insisted that the consecrated bread and wine must be regarded only as symbols, or "representations," of the Lord's body and blood.

However, the greatest gulf between Lutheranism and Calvinism did not stem from any particular doctrine, but rather from entirely different attitudes toward life. Luther loved life, and believed that men should enjoy thankfully all God's gifts, from the beauty of a sunset to the conviviality of a temperate glass of beer. Calvin, by contrast, was an apostle of austerity. He abhorred all kinds of frivolity, and called on men to turn their attention away from the snares and illusions of this life and concentrate wholly on serving God and preparing for the other world. "Either the earth must become vile in our estimation," he said, "or it will retain our immoderate love." Dour and ascetic by temperament, Calvin left the lasting imprint of his personality on a large area of Protestantism in the form of continuing attitudes toward drinking, dancing, card-playing, Sunday amusements, and other "frivolities."

Although Calvin's teachings have influenced many branches of Protestantism, there is one big denominational family that can claim, more accurately than any other, to be descended from the Geneva reformer. It is the second largest of the great Protestant confessions, with nearly 70 million members throughout the world. Its constituents are known in Continental Europe as "Reformed churches." In Scotland and the United States they are known as Presbyterian churches.

The Origin of "Presbyterian"

Presbyterians trace their lineage to Calvin through the Scottish reformer John Knox, who was one of Calvin's disciples in Geneva. Knox changed little of Calvin's theology in adapting it to the British Isles, from which it was shortly to immigrate to America. What he did contribute was a well-conceived system of church government—the so-called Presbyterian polity—from which the Scottish and American branches of the Reformed church family take their name.

The term Presbyterian comes from the Greek word *presbuteros*, meaning elder. Each local congregation, called a *session*, is governed by two kinds of elders: teaching elders, who correspond to the ordained ministers of other Protestant bodies; and ruling elders, who are laymen elected by the congregation, much as Baptists elect deacons, or as Episcopalians elect vestrymen.

Although a session has considerable autonomy in handling its local affairs, it is not independent. Every session in a city or other appropriate geographical area is under the jurisdiction of the *presbytery* for that area. The presbytery is made up of two representatives from each session —one teaching elder and one ruling elder; in other words, one minister and one layman.

The presbyteries in turn are united in *synods*, and the synods in a General Assembly that covers the entire nation. These are representative bodies exactly like the presbytery. Presbyterians believe that this system of church government has several advantages. It provides for firm central authority without vesting it in a single individual, such as a bishop. It gives laymen an equal voice with the clergy in all important policy decisions. On the other hand, it avoids the dangers of demagoguery and a stampeded majority that might attend the pure democracy of a church governed by congregational vote. It is government by elected representatives, and if it reminds one of the system set up by the U. S. Constitution, it is no mere coincidence. There were many Presbyterians among the Founding Fathers.

The American Presbyterians

The first Presbyterian church on American soil was established at Jamestown, Virginia, in 1611. During the colonial era, Presbyterian strength centered in the middle colonies —New York, New Jersey, Pennsylvania, Delaware, and

Maryland—which attracted large numbers of Scotch-Irish immigrants. It was a Scotch-Irish missionary, Francis Makemie, who in 1705 organized the first presbytery in the American colonies.

Over the next two centuries, Presbyterianism in America was rent by several schisms. The biggest one resulted from the Civil War and is still reflected in the existence of the Presbyterian Church in the United States, better known as the Southern Presbyterian Church, which is the second largest Presbyterian body in the United States, with 900,000 members.

The largest is the United Presbyterian Church in the U.S.A., which has well over 3 million members. There are eight other Presbyterian denominations, ranging in size from the Cumberland Presbyterian Church with 90,000 members to the Associate Presbyterian Church of North America, which claims fewer than 500. Many of the smaller Presbyterian bodies are Fundamentalist in doctrine, and split away from the "U.S.A." Church during the theological controversies of the 1920s and 1930s.

The Order of Worship

Presbyterians place great store by orderliness. If they have a favorite biblical verse, it is St. Paul's admonition: "Let everything be done decently and in order." This passion for propriety is reflected in their services of worship, which are plain, simple, and dignified. Like many other Protestant bodies, Presbyterians have been moving in recent years in the direction of a richer liturgy, with greater emphasis on the service of Holy Communion; but the principal service in Presbyterian churches continues to be the "service of the Word," built around Scripture readings, prayers, hymns, and a sermon, with the latter occupying the center of interest.

Presbyterian ministers often wear black academic robes with little white collars called "Geneva tabs." Some, however, wear cassocks in church, and there are a few who dare to wear round collars despite their "Roman" associations.

There is great doctrinal variation among the local churches of the United Presbyterian Church. In one you may encounter a pastor who is a way-out theological liberal, and in the next, one who is an unabashed Fundamentalist. If there is any theological viewpoint that can be said to represent the mainstream of this denomination, however, it is Modern Orthodoxy. Southern Presbyterian churches tend to be somewhat more conservative.

Presbyterians have taken an active part in civic affairs ever since colonial times. In any legislative body, from a city council to the U. S. Congress, you will find a disproportionate number of Presbyterians. Generally speaking, Presbyterian churches attract an upper-middle-class constituency. A Presbyterian family magazine learned from a survey of its subscribers that 84 per cent owned their own homes, 54 per cent had attended college, 29 per cent were in the learned professions, and 12 per cent were business executives. Perhaps even more than the Episcopal Church, Presbyterian churches have become the "status" churches of the suburbs.

Despite their relatively privileged backgrounds, Presbyterians have displayed a strong social conscience, particularly on racial issues. No other Protestant denomination has fought for Negro equality more courageously and uncompromisingly.

THE ANGLICANS

The Anglican Communion is a world-wide fellowship of some 40 million Christians, the third oldest and third largest family of Reformation churches. It is composed of the Church of England and seventeen other autonomous national churches, including the Protestant Episcopal Church in the United States, that are historically descended from it.

If you want to irritate an Anglican friend, tell him that Henry VIII founded the Church of England because he wanted a divorce. There is just enough truth in this ancient jibe to make it really annoying. But it is a serious oversimplification of history.

The Reformation would have come to England even if Henry had been completely satisfied with his marriage to the Spanish princess Catherine of Aragon. Two centuries before Luther nailed his theses to the church door in Wittenberg, the Oxford don John Wycliffe was translating the Bible into English, denying the supreme authority of the Pope, and proclaiming the priesthood of all believers. By the early sixteenth century, when the Continental reformers broke with Rome, the religious ferment in England was so strong that one church functionary complained of a shortage of wood with which to burn heretics.

The heretic-burning was done at the instigation of Henry VIII, who displayed such zeal for Catholicism that the Vatican awarded him the title "Defender of the Faith." Henry's zeal began to flag, however, when his Spanish queen failed to give him a male heir to the throne, and Pope Clement VII refused to grant an annulment of the marriage. Henry felt, with considerable justification, that the Pope's refusal was not based on religious scruples, of which Clement VII had shown precious few on any other matters, but rather stemmed from the circumstance of the Pope's being a virtual prisoner of Emperor Charles V, who was a nephew of Catherine of Aragon.

Henry responded by repudiating the authority of the Pope, and proclaiming himself the head of the Church in England. This action—ratified by an act of Parliament in 1534—was all the Reformation that Henry wanted, and all that he permitted. Until his death in 1547, English churches remained rigorously Catholic in doctrine and worship.

The Book of Common Prayer

When Henry's nine-year-old son, Edward VI, came to the throne, the English Reformation became something more than a political adjustment. Under the leadership of Thomas Cranmer, Archbishop of Canterbury, English reformers purged the Mass of medieval accretions and translated it into an English-language service of Holy Communion. They also simplified other services and made them available in the language of the people. The service manual which they compiled was called The Prayer-Book of King Edward VI. It was the first version of the famous Book of Common Prayer, which is universally recognized as the greatest liturgical treasure of the English language, and which is still used in Anglican churches throughout the world.

Edward VI died at the age of fifteen, and was succeeded on the throne by his half sister, Mary Tudor, an ardent Catholic who was determined to restore English obedience to the Pope. She burned, beheaded, and hanged hundreds of church leaders, including Archbishop Cranmer, in pursuit of this pious intent. Although she fully earned her nickname "Bloody Mary," she succeeded only in alienating the sympathies of the people and she left England far more Protestant in spirit than she found it.

Mary was followed by the great Queen Elizabeth I. This astute young woman, daughter of Henry VIII and Anne Boleyn, restored her father's Act of Supremacy—making the English sovereign rather than the Roman Pope head of the Church in England—which had been repealed under Mary. Elizabeth also decreed that all English churches must use the services provided in Archbishop Cranmer's prayer book. Bishops who refused to accept Elizabeth as head of the Church in England were removed from office without fanfare or martyrdom. The whole thing was done so quietly and smoothly that it was not until 1570—twelve years after Elizabeth came to the throne—that Pope Pius V published a bull excommunicating Elizabeth and all English bishops and priests who had accepted her as head of the English Church.

Under Elizabeth and her Archbishop of Canterbury, Matthew Parker, the Church of England was increasingly receptive to the Protestant doctrines emanating from Luther's Germany and Calvin's Geneva. The Thirty-nine Articles of Religion adopted in Elizabeth's reign as a doctrinal yardstick for the Church of England are distinctly Protestant in tone. They affirm the sufficiency of the Scriptures as a source of Christian teaching, and declare that men are justified by faith alone. The number of sacraments is reduced from the seven recognized by the Roman Catholic Church to the two which the New Testament records as having been instituted by Christ—baptism and Holy Communion. They support Luther's doctrine that Christ is actually present in the sacrament of Holy Communion, but reject the Catholic doctrine of transubstantiation as "repugnant to the plain words of Scripture." The "Romish doctrine" of purgatory, with its related beliefs in the granting of indulgences and pardons by the Church and the invocation of saints, is dismissed as "a fond thing, vainly invented, and grounded upon no warranty of Scripture."

Are Anglicans Protestant or Catholic?

Despite the almost truculently Protestant tenor of the Thirty-nine Articles, which are still published in the back of every Book of Common Prayer, many Anglicans from the sixteenth century until the present have bridled at being called Protestants. They prefer to think of themselves as members of a reformed Catholic church—one which has retained the ancient Catholic creeds and the true Catholic sacraments, and which has preserved a threefold ministry of bishops, priests, and deacons who can trace their line of ordination back to the Apostles. The claim of "Apostolic succession" for Anglican clergymen is based on the fact that the Church of England did not acquire a new ministry at the time of its establishment: it continued under the same bishops and priests it had before its break with Rome. Anglicans contend that the Vatican itself tacitly recognized the validity of Anglican orders when it waited twelve years to excommunicate the clergymen who acknowledged Elizabeth as head of the Church of England.

The Anglican attempt to retain what is valid in Catholic tradition while accepting the basic insights of the Protestant reformer is a typically English solution. It is the English genius for compromise applied to religion. Some people find the result distasteful: they dismiss Anglicanism as being neither Catholic fish nor Protestant fowl. But others agree with the noted Anglican scholar Dr. Chad Walsh:

"If Christendom is ever to be reunited into one great Church, that Church will of necessity be one with sufficient scope and flexibility to find room for what is best in both the Protestant and Catholic traditions. I believe the Anglican Communion is a small-scale model of what such a Church can be."

It is an indisputable fact that the Anglican Communion has succeeded for more than four hundred years in holding together in one body "Anglo-Catholics," whose worship is virtually indistinguishable from the Roman Mass; "high churchmen," who emphasize the Catholic heritage; "low churchmen," who lean more toward the Protestant tradition; "evangelicals," who are hard to tell from campmeeting Protestants; and finally—most numerous of all— "broad churchmen," who cherish both the Catholic and the Protestant aspects of the Anglican *via media,* and who welcome the opportunity to serve as a bridge between the divided branches of the Christian family.

Their commitment to the cause of Christian reunion has prompted Anglicans to play a leading role in such ecumenical organizations as the World Council of Churches. When Rome began to show signs of greater openness toward the "separated brethren," Anglicans were quick to respond. It was the Archbishop of Canterbury who first paid a courtesy call on Pope John XXIII—blazing a trail that many Protestant church leaders were to follow.

Episcopalians—the American Anglicans

In the United States, the Episcopal Church was a charter member of the Consultation on Church Union, formed in 1961 to explore the possibility of merging six major denominations into a 20-million-member church that would be "truly catholic, truly reformed, and truly evangelical."

The Episcopal Church, like the Presbyterian churches, derived its name from the way it is governed. *Episkopos* is the Greek word for "bishop." Episcopal bishops have no more actual power than have the administrative officers of most Protestant bodies. Their wishes in such matters as the handling of money and the management of church-related institutions are subject to the action of democratically elected bodies representative of the church membership. Also, local congregations retain a large degree of autonomy. But Episcopalians do not look upon their bishops primarily as administrative officers. They are the spiritual shepherds of the flock, true successors to the Apostles, commissioned in the name of Christ to ordain the clergy and confirm the laity, charged with preserving sound doctrine and interpreting the teachings of Christ.

This view of the episcopate is shared by all the Anglican churches. It is essentially a "catholic" view and is one of the most important things that Anglicans have in common with the Roman and Eastern Orthodox communions. Several Protestant bodies—for example, America's Methodists and some European Lutheran churches—use the title of bishop, but their bishops are administrative officers and are not regarded as possessing special apostolic powers in the spiritual realm.

Anglicanism came to America with the earliest English settlers. The first Anglican church was established at Jamestown, Virginia, in 1607 by a chaplain who accompanied Captain John Smith's party. Before the Revolution, Anglicanism was the established state religion of most of the Southern colonies, supported by tax revenues. George Washington, James Madison, Alexander Hamilton, Patrick Henry, and many other Founding Fathers were Anglicans.

During the Revolution, the Anglican churches lost many of their English-bred clergymen, who were appalled at the way the colonials were carrying on and took themselves home to London. They also suffered from popular resentment against a church that recognized George III as its official head. When the Revolutionary War began in 1776, the Anglican churches comprised the largest religious body in America. When it ended, they were one of the smallest.

The slow job of rebuilding began in 1783, when Anglican clergymen in Connecticut held a meeting and elected one of their number, the Reverend Samuel Seabury of Groton, to be their bishop. Seabury went to England to seek consecration from the mother church, but the English bishops subjected him to such a runaround that he finally went up to Scotland, where he duly received the laying-on of hands from three bishops of the Anglican Church of Scotland. Two other American clergymen, William White, of Philadelphia, and Samuel Provoost, of New York, later received consecration as bishops in England. In 1789 Bishop White presided at a general convocation of Anglicans, at which the Protestant Episcopal Church in the United States was formally established.

The growth of the Episcopal Church was slow for many years following the Revolution. In the areas where it had once enjoyed established status, it had a hard time teaching its members to support church activities by voluntary contributions. English-oriented even after the Revolution, it continued to hug the Eastern seaboard, and neglected to evangelize the frontier, where other Protestant bodies were making tremendous strides. It acquired a reputation as a church that catered to the carriage trade and had no room for the masses—a reputation it is still trying valiantly to live down.

By the start of World War I, more than three centuries after the first Anglican service of worship was conducted at Jamestown, the Episcopal Church had only one million members, 85 per cent of whom were concentrated in the East and South.

It was not until after World War II that the Episcopal Church finally shook off the lethargy that had earned it the nickname of "God's frozen people." The postwar boom in church membership came along just as Episcopalians were awakening to the fact that Jesus was speaking to them too when He said that the gospel must be preached "to every living creature." Episcopalians began showing evangelistic zeal just as millions of Americans began looking around for a church, and from the coinciding of these factors came a rapid spurt in growth. Between 1950 and 1960, the membership of the Episcopal Church almost doubled. Today it is one of the six largest American denominations, with more than 3.3 million members. Among them are people from every race, nationality, and economic group—living refutations of the old "class church" label.

The Episcopal Appeal

If the Episcopal Church still has a special appeal for any one group of Americans, it is for the academic-intellectual-professional community. Large numbers of scientists, doctors, lawyers, writers, college professors, and the like, are to be found in the pews of Episcopal churches.

One reason is that Episcopal clergymen are notably well educated, and their sermons rarely if ever insult the intelligence of any listener, however learned he may be.

Episcopalians probably do not drink any more than the members of some Protestant churches that are officially committed to total abstinence; but they are less furtive about it. The Episcopal Church condemns any use of alcohol that leads to drunkenness or impairs a person's ability to discharge his responsibilities, but sees no sin in moderate drinking at an appropriate time and place.

Episcopalians also take a relaxed attitude toward card-playing, dancing, Sunday golf, and other social activities that cause the blood pressure of a strict Calvinist to rise.

This should not be taken, however, as indicating a laissez-faire attitude toward moral issues. No other non-Roman church takes such a dim view of divorce as does the Episcopal Church. And Episcopalians have been in the front ranks of the fight for racial justice.

To outsiders, the most conspicuous virtue of the Episcopal Church is the beauty of its liturgy. Although many other churches have borrowed liberally from the Book of Common Prayer, its majestic cadences still sound most at home in an Episcopal setting. If you have never heard a good choir leading an Episcopal congregation in the Venite, or a strong-voiced Episcopal priest standing before the altar to open the Communion service with the Prayer for the Whole State of Christ's Church, you do not know how poetic and uplifting corporate worship can be.

Episcopalians know. And that's why they tend to be almost fanatically devoted to their church.

CHAPTER VI

The Puritan Heritage

The English Reformation was a compromise, and like most compromises, it left many people dissatisfied. The Church of England as it emerged under Queen Elizabeth I was too Calvinist for strict Catholics and too Catholic for strict Calvinists. The Catholic protest was climaxed by the bull of excommunication issued by Pope Pius V in 1570. The Calvinist protest was expressed in the Puritan movement, which kept England in turmoil for a century, exerted a mighty influence on the colonization of America, and led directly to the establishment of two great new Protestant denominations.

The term "Puritan" was applied to all-out Protestants who wanted to "purify" the Church of England of Catholic influences. The poet John Milton, who was an ardent Puritan, described Puritanism as a drive to "reform the Reformation"—to carry the break with Rome to its logical conclusion. The Puritans were true spiritual sons of John Calvin—earnest, austere, suspicious of the comforts and pleasures of this world, fired with a great sense of rectitude and a conviction of their own "election" as children of God.

By 1563—five years after Elizabeth came to the throne —the Puritans constituted a sufficiently strong faction within the established Church of England to challenge its policies openly. They first voiced "scruples" on a relatively trivial matter—the kind of vestments worn by the clergy. Soon they were protesting against a whole range of "Romanish" practices—kneeling at Communion, the use of the sign of the cross in baptism, the observance of holy days. In 1580 they went a significant step further and denounced the whole idea of a hierarchical church governed by bishops. Instead, they said, each congregation should manage its own affairs, and elect its own minister.

The Church of England, backed by Elizabeth's government, reacted by imposing heavy penalties on "nonconformists." More than two hundred ministers were suspended for involvement with the Puritan movement, and about seventy were sent to prison. These acts of repression merely stimulated the movement, and when James I succeeded Elizabeth on the throne of England, near the end of the sixteenth century, Puritanism was a thriving force in English religious life.

James I was a notoriously pigheaded man, even by the high standards of English royalty. He crushed every hope of an accommodation that would have permitted the Puritans to remain within the Church of England, and, with a public promise to "harry them out of the land," launched a ruthless persecution.

Many of the Puritans fled to Holland. This exodus was an event of far-reaching importance in religious history.

Two major Protestant groups—the Congregationalists and the Baptists—can trace their origins to congregations of English Puritans living in exile in Holland.

THE CONGREGATIONALISTS

Although Holland granted religious freedom to the Puritans, it could not provide all of them with homes and jobs. By 1620 the plight of the transplanted Puritans had become bad enough to make them willing to undertake a dangerous adventure. A little band of men and women from the Puritan congregation at Leyden, Holland, returned briefly to England, and on September 6, 1620, sailed from the port of Plymouth in a frail 180-ton ship named the *Mayflower*. They were bound for Virginia, where they had received a grant of land. But their tiny ship was blown far off course by North Atlantic gales, and they arrived instead in Massachusetts. They disembarked at Plymouth Rock, and promptly began building a church.

The Pilgrims

This first batch of Puritan colonists—who are known in our history books as "the Pilgrims" (for no good reason except to make things more difficult for school children) —were soon followed by others. By 1640, more than twenty thousand Puritans had emigrated from England to the rocky and inhospitable wilderness which they named "New England."

They were stern, hardy people, full of religious zeal. The churches they established were strictly "congregational" in government—which is to say that all questions, including the choice of a minister, were settled democratically, with each member of the congregation having an equal vote. Because of this distinctive form of church government, they came to be known in America as "Congregationalists."

In their eagerness to purge all remnants of "papalism" from their churches, the Congregationalists adopted a severely simple form of worship, built around Scripture readings and interminably long sermons. (Some of the famous colonial preachers—Cotton Mather, for one—considered a two-hour sermon a relatively brief homily.) The austerity of the Congregational liturgy was reflected in the rigorously plain architecture of the churches in which it was housed. Everyone who has seen a New England village in the autumn must be forever grateful that the Puritan conscience permitted the addition of high steeples, which were considered acceptable adornment because they pointed upward toward God. To squelch any possible scruple about vain display, however, the steeples were also given a functional use as bell-towers, for summoning the faithful to church.

Although they had come to America seeking religious freedom for themselves, the Congregationalists were not keen on granting it to others. They accorded "established" status to their own churches, and did not hesitate to use the power of civil government to achieve their religious ends. Only Congregationalists in good standing were permitted to vote in civil elections in the Massachusetts Bay Colony. Everyone was taxed for support of the Church, and those who failed to attend a worship service were subject to punishment by the civil government. Sabbath observance was enforced by civil statute—the first "blue laws."

During the colonial era, Congregationalism dominated New England, while Anglicanism dominated the Southern colonies. The Revolution led to the discrediting and virtual collapse of Anglicanism, and Congregationalism emerged from the struggle for independence as the most powerful religious body in America.

The Congregational Stamp on American Life

Congregationalists have placed their stamp on American life in many different ways. Their concept of democratic government is reflected in our basic political system. Their harvest festival of thanksgiving to God (which they adapted from Old Testament accounts of the Jewish feast of Succoth) survives, in name at least, in the national holiday now dedicated to turkey dinners and football games. Their concern for education is enshrined in such Congregationalist-founded institutions as Harvard, Yale, Dartmouth, Williams, Amherst, Oberlin, Mount Holyoke, Smith, and Wellesley.

Two other Congregationalist concerns have had a tremendous influence on religious life in America. They are foreign missions and Negro rights.

The first missionary ever sent out by an American church was the Reverend Thomas Mayhew, a Congregationalist who started preaching to the Indians on Martha's Vineyard island in 1641. A few years later another Congregationalist missionary, the Reverend John Eliot, translated the Bible into the language of the Algonquin Indians. It was the first Bible printed in the American colonies.

In 1806 a group of students at Williams College formed America's first missionary society. It came to be known as the American Board of Commissioners for Foreign Missions, and it pioneered the great movement of American foreign missionaries into Hawaii, India, China, and South America during the nineteenth century. It is still active, operating hundreds of schools, colleges, hospitals, clinics, leprosariums, and providing "fraternal support" to thousands of indigenous Christian churches in twenty-five countries.

During the decades preceding the Civil War, such Congregationalist ministers as Henry Ward Beecher led the movement for the abolition of slavery. Determination to win social justice for Negroes has continued to be a strong Congregationalist tradition into our own day.

Although insisting on the autonomy of the local church, Congregationalists recognized the value of cooperation in such projects as supporting missionaries and founding colleges. Early in the nineteenth century they began forming "associations" on a local and state basis. In 1871 a national association was founded, the National Council of Congregational Churches, which in 1931 merged with the General Convention of the Christian Church to form the Congregational Christian Churches.

The United Church of Christ

In 1957 the Congregational Christian Churches merged with the Evangelical and Reformed Church, a Calvinist body formed during the colonial era by German and Dutch immigrants to Pennsylvania. The new denomination is called The United Church of Christ. With a membership of more than 2 million, it is the nation's seventh largest Protestant body.

Modern Congregationalists are rarely "puritanical" in their attitudes toward dancing, card-playing, Sunday observance, and so on. Many of them bend over backward to demonstrate their open-mindedness on questions of private morality. Although their churches are still officially Calvinist in theology, they have carried to its logical conclusion the doctrine that each individual is free to interpret the Scriptures for himself. There is no creed, no set of beliefs or doctrines, that a person must embrace in order to become a Congregationalist. Thus one encounters in Congregationalist (or United) churches a great latitude of belief, ranging from Calvinist orthodoxy to way-out theological liberalism.

THE BAPTISTS

According to Baptist folklore, the Baptist movement originated with John the Baptist, who baptized Jesus and others in the River Jordan. Without denying this claim— a bold thing to do in the presence of an ardent Baptist— church historians point out that the first record of a church congregation calling itself "Baptist" is found in Holland in the year 1609. It was established by a group of Puritans who had fled from England under the leadership of John Smyth. While in Holland, they were attracted to some of the doctrines of a group of Protestants known as Anabaptists, who were the forerunners of the modern Mennonites (who are discussed at greater length in the next chapter).

The Anabaptists

The Anabaptists condemned infant baptism, which was then practiced almost universally by Protestants as well as Catholics. They held that baptism is not a sacrament in the sense understood by Catholics and most Protestants —that is, an outward rite in which divine grace is mystically imparted to a human soul—but is rather a kind of testimonial of faith, in which a believer in Christ bears witness to his own conversion and is initiated into the fellowship of the Christian community. Thus, they said, baptism can have no meaning unless it is restricted to those who are old enough to make a mature "decision for Christ." They also insisted that baptism must be by total immersion of the body—the method which the New Testament indicates was used in the baptism of Jesus— rather than by the pouring or sprinkling methods which most other Christian bodies have adopted as a symbolic substitute for immersion.

The Baptist congregation founded by John Smyth and his followers in Holland took over this Anabaptist doctrine of baptism, and grafted it onto a Puritan-Calvinist theology that emphasized congregational autonomy, reverence for the Bible as the sole source of Christian teaching, and the competence of each individual soul to gain direct access to God without the mediation of any priest or minister.

America's Debt to Roger Williams

Although the Baptist movement grew slowly in Holland, and gained a foothold across the Channel in England, it was in America that it finally found fertile soil. The first Baptist church in the new world was founded in 1639 by the Reverend Roger Williams, a Church of England priest who had cast his lot with the Puritans and fled to Massachusetts under threat of imprisonment. But Williams found the established Congregational Church of the colony every bit as intolerant as the state church that had stifled his spirit back home in England. He particularly disapproved the assessment of taxes to support Congregational churches, and the use of civil law to enforce church discipline. Again threatened with imprisonment or deportation, he left Boston in 1636 and took refuge among the Narragansett Indians. From them, he secured title to a piece of land that is the present site of Providence, Rhode Island. Other discontented colonists joined him there, and in 1639 they baptized one another by immersion and formed America's first Baptist congregation.

The founders of the Baptist colony in Rhode Island were unique in that they treasured religious liberty for others as well as for themselves. They drew up a compact that provided for absolute freedom of religion and a strict separation of church and state. This concept, now enshrined in the First Amendment to the Constitution, is one of the most precious aspects of America's heritage. Under it, religion has thrived in this nation as it has never done in any country with an established state church. All

American denominations now look upon religious liberty as a blessing—and we owe it primarily to the Baptists who followed Roger Williams into the wilds.

The Baptist movement remained relatively small throughout the colonial era. But with the coming of independence, and especially with the opening of the Western frontier, it began to grow explosively. The local Baptist church, governed by its own members, free to elect and ordain its own pastor, totally independent of any ecclesiastical organization, proved highly attractive to the freedom-loving men of the frontier. The preaching in Baptist churches was often more fiery than profound, since a congregation could ordain to the ministry any man who felt he had a divine call to preach, however little education or preparation he might have had. But Baptists were not greatly troubled by a lack of learning among their pastors: they were convinced that the Bible itself contained all the "saving truth" that any man needed to know, and that each man was required to "work out his own salvation" by reading the Scriptures and by making a personal commitment of faith in Jesus Christ. The emphasis on personal faith led, inevitably, to a preoccupation with a felt experience of conversion. And this led, in turn, to emotion-filled "revival meetings" and to the tradition of concluding each Sunday service with an "invitation" to repentant sinners to come forward and declare their faith in Christ.

The Baptist Groups Today

Today, the Baptists constitute America's largest Protestant family by a wide margin. There are approximately 23 million of them. They are grouped into twenty-eight different associations, conferences, or conventions (Baptists do not like the term denomination). At first glance, this may seem like a high degree of fragmentation. But the real marvel is that ninety thousand local Baptist churches—each a law unto itself and fiercely jealous of its independence—have been able to coalesce into as few as twenty-eight organizations.

The largest Baptist body, and the largest single Protestant organization in America, is the Southern Baptist Convention. Formed in Augusta, Georgia, in 1845, it remained largely a regional body until about 1940. Since then, however, it has far outgrown the boundaries implied by its name. There are now "Southern" Baptist churches in all fifty states. California, for example, has nearly a thousand. Nationwide, the Southern Baptist Convention has more than 10 million members.

Southern Baptists are uncompromising Fundamentalists in theology. They will fire a seminary professor who suggests that the creation story in Genesis is a religious parable, and is not meant to be read as a literal scientific account of what took place during the first seven days of the world's existence.

Their rigorous conservatism in doctrine has made them wary of contacts with other denominations (including other Baptist groups), which are, in their view, gravely tainted with liberalism. They have accordingly remained aloof from such cooperative organizations as the National and World Council of Churches, and have refused even to discuss possible mergers.

The American Baptist Convention, which used to be

called the Northern Baptist Convention, is considerably smaller, with slightly more than 1.5 million members. Some of its churches are Fundamentalist, but many are receptive to the viewpoints of Modern Orthodoxy or Liberalism. The American Baptists are very active in the National Council of Churches and other cooperative Protestant bodies.

Two other large Baptist bodies are predominantly Negro in their membership. The National Baptist Convention of the U.S.A., Inc. claims 5 million members. The National Baptist Convention of America reports 2.7 million.

In addition to these four giants, which account for more than 90 per cent of the nation's Baptists, there are Seventh-Day Baptists, who worship on Saturday instead of Sunday; Primitive Baptists, who conduct foot-washing ceremonies as part of each celebration of the Lord's Supper; Free-Will (or Free) Baptists, who stress man's freedom to choose salvation or perdition; Predestinarian Baptists, who cling to Calvin's doctrine of the double election; and many other varieties.

Despite their differences over doctrinal details, Baptists of all types are united in their insistence on "believer's baptism" by total immersion. They also have in common a fierce devotion to the principle of church-state separation, which they defend with great vigor through a highly effective Washington lobby called the Baptist Joint Committee on Public Affairs. Baptists frequently suspect Roman Catholics of trying to undermine the "wall of separation" and raid the public treasury. For this reason and others, anti-Catholic sentiments are more pronounced among Baptists than in almost any other Protestant group.

(The Baptist World Alliance was the only major Protestant body that rejected the invitation to send observers to the Vatican Ecumenical Council.)

Among the issues that divide Baptists, none has a higher emotional voltage than segregation. Negro Baptists and Northern white Baptists are committed to the elimination of racial barriers. Southern Baptists have had great travail of conscience on this question, and with a few notable exceptions, Baptist churches in the South have tended either to sit out the desegregation fight, or passively defend the *status quo*.

Baptists are great supporters of foreign missions. The Southern Baptist Convention alone maintains more than 1500 full-time missionaries abroad. They also are zealous evangelizers at home, conducting house-to-house visitation drives to reach unchurched families. The greatest practitioner of mass evangelism of our time, the Reverend Billy Graham, is a Baptist.

In recent years, Baptists have made a mighty effort to upgrade the educational level of their clergy. You may still encounter an "ordained amateur" in the pulpit of a small-town or rural Baptist church, but elsewhere today you are much more likely to find seminary-educated ministers.

How Baptists Worship

Baptist worship is traditionally informal: a typical service includes spontaneous prayers, Scripture reading, hymn-singing, and the sermon, followed by the pastor's invitation for converts to come forward.

The Lord's Supper is observed at least four times a year,

with grape juice instead of wine, and small cubes of ordinary loaf bread instead of the flat Communion wafers familiar to Catholics, Anglicans, Lutherans, and others. The elements are passed around the pews by deacons, and members of the congregation receive them while remaining in their seats instead of coming forward to kneel at an altar rail. To Baptists, the observance is strictly an "ordinance"—that is, a memorial to Jesus—rather than a sacrament with mystical power to convey grace.

Baptist ministers customarily wear business suits rather than gowns or any other type of clerical vestment. There is no altar in a Baptist church. The pulpit dominates the interior architecture. Behind the choir section, usually, there is a tank about four feet deep which can be filled with water for baptism by immersion. In some rural areas, baptisms are still performed in a river, just as they were by John the Baptist nearly two thousand years ago.

CHAPTER VII

More Movements Born of the Church of England

In the early eighteenth century, Puritanism was thriving in the American colonies. But it was a spent force in the mother country, and the Church of England had once again lapsed into that state of sterile complacency that is the peculiar pitfall of established churches. It was time for a new prophet to arise.

THE METHODISTS

He was born in 1703, the fifteenth of nineteen children sired by the busy Anglican rector of Epworth, England. His name was John Wesley, and he deserves a place on any list of the great religious leaders of history. Had he been born a couple of centuries sooner, he doubtless would have ranked with Luther and Calvin as a Father of the Reformation. A century earlier, he would have been a Puritan. In his own time, he became the founder of Methodism.

It is ironic that the term "Methodist," now universally associated with the movement initiated by Wesley, actually

stemmed from an early experiment in religious life that
Wesley tried and found wanting.

While he was at Oxford University, preparing for the
Anglican ministry, Wesley became the leader of a little
band of students who sought spiritual renewal through
methodical diligence in study and worship. They arranged
a strict daily schedule of duties, with fixed hours for visit-
ing the sick, conducting schools among the poor, and
preaching to those in prison. They prayed aloud three
times a day and stopped for silent prayer every hour on
the hour.

Other Oxford students made fun of them, and expressed
their contempt in a variety of derisive nicknames for the
group, including "The Bible Moths," "The Holy Club,"
and "The Methodists."

The latter label stuck, and continued to follow Wesley
long after he had concluded that man does not achieve
peace with God through rules and stringent efforts at self-
perfection.

The Aldersgate Experience

The turning point in Wesley's life came on the evening
of May 24, 1738. He attended a prayer meeting at a little
chapel on Aldersgate Street in London. As he sat in meditation, listening to someone read aloud from Luther's
writings, Wesley suddenly knew what Luther meant when
he insisted that men are saved through faith in Christ
alone, and not by any good works of their own.

"I felt my heart strangely warmed," Wesley wrote later.

"I felt I did trust in Christ, Christ alone, for salvation; and an assurance was given me that He had taken away my sins, even mine. . . ."

From that moment on, Wesley was a different man. Before the "heart-warming experience," he had been an ascetic, scholarly Anglican priest—to put it baldly, a self-righteous prig. Afterwards he became a generous, outgoing man, fired by a passionate desire to share with others his great discovery that salvation is God's free gift.

For the next fifty years, John Wesley preached this good news throughout England. When churches were closed to him—as they often were—he held his meetings in open fields. His sermons often drew as many as 30,000 persons. It has been calculated that Wesley traveled 250,000 miles on his evangelistic missions, and that he delivered 42,000 sermons—an average of two each weekday and four every Sunday for half a century.

Although the Wesleyan revival brought badly needed new life into the Church of England, the leaders of that incredibly durable but often obtuse institution predictably turned up their noses at the whole thing. They refused ordination to the corps of young lay preachers whom Wesley had recruited to help him. Had they been less stubborn on this point, it is entirely possible that the Methodist movement would have remained inside the Anglican Communion as Wesley himself did to his dying day.

The ordination conflict came to a head when Wesley's "Methodist societies" spread to the American colonies. By the end of the Revolution, there were fifteen thousand Methodists in America, and they had no ordained clergymen to care for them. Wesley made a final appeal to the bishops of the Church of England to ordain some priests for missionary service among American Methodists. When it was refused, he took the fateful step of ordaining two men, on his own initiative, to "preside over the flock in America."

Since the Church of England never recognized the validity of these and subsequent Methodist ordinations, the Wesleyan movement from that time forward was a separate denomination.

This practical fact, which Wesley chose to ignore, was recognized by the American Methodists, who held a conference at Baltimore in 1784 and formally organized The Methodist Episcopal Church.

The Circuit Riders

Wesley's evangelistic zeal was faithfully reflected by the "circuit-riding" preachers of American Methodism. While the Congregationalists and Episcopalians snuggled close to the Eastern seaboard, the Methodists set out to preach the gospel to the raw communities of the burgeoning frontier. The first Methodist bishop in the United States, Dr. Francis Asbury, set an example by traveling some 275,000 miles on horseback to pass out Bibles, conduct revival meetings, and perform baptisms and marriages.

From the start, Methodists attached great importance to what they called "a felt experience of salvation." They believed that every man should be able, like John Wesley, to recall the very hour and moment when he knew himself to be saved through faith in Christ. This emphasis on conversion as a dramatic experience naturally led to a highly emotional atmosphere at Methodist revival meetings. And Methodist preachers contributed to it by including plenty of fire-and-brimstone in their sermons.

The simple, uneducated people of the frontier found this approach to religion highly congenial. They flocked into the Methodist Church in such great numbers that by the time of the Civil War, Abraham Lincoln spoke of it as the largest and "most important" denomination in America.

To a greater degree than any other Protestant denomination, Methodism is the "lengthened shadow" of the remarkable man who founded it. Virtually every distinctive trait of the Methodist movement can be traced back to John Wesley himself. We have already noted how this is true in the case of Methodist emphasis on "felt salvation" and in the tradition of evangelistic vigor. But it is equally true of other Methodist characteristics.

The Efficient Organizers

For example, Wesley was a great organizer. The historian Macaulay once compared his organizing genius to that of Richelieu. And the Methodist Church remains perhaps the most efficiently organized of all Protestant bodies.

Methodist congregations are organized into districts, with a superintendent in charge of each district. Districts are formed into annual conferences, often along state lines.

Two or more annual conferences comprise an episcopal area, under the direction of a bishop. Annual conferences are grouped into jurisdictions.*

Above the jurisdictions is the General Conference, the top legislative body of American Methodism. Composed of equal numbers of lay and clerical delegates, it meets every four years, and provides Methodists with the same kind of representative voice in the Church's government that an American citizen has in Congress.

The key man in the Methodist set-up is the bishop. A Methodist bishop has far more administrative power than an Episcopal bishop. It might even be argued that he wields greater power than a Roman Catholic bishop, since he does not have the Roman Curia looking over his shoulder and meddling in his most routine decisions. The Methodist bishop's vast authority stems in large part from his power to determine which minister shall serve which congregation. All ministerial appointments are subject to change annually, which means that every Methodist minister is at the mercy of his bishop, either in remaining at a church he likes, or in being transferred to a more desirable assignment. There is no danger of a congregation seceding from the denomination if it doesn't like the bishop's decision: the title to all church property is vested

* There are six Methodist jurisdictions in the United States. Five are purely regional, but the so-called "Central Jurisdiction" is a segregated racial unit, set up to include annual conferences of Negro Methodists in all parts of the country. The Central Jurisdiction has become a great embarrassment to Methodists in recent years, and the Church is moving toward its elimination by incorporating Negro congregations and conferences into the regular regional jurisdictions as rapidly as this can be accomplished.

in the central organization rather than the local congregation.

This system of organization is, as stated above, unquestionably efficient. And many Methodist bishops use their power carefully and conscientiously for the good of the whole church. But wherever there is great power, there are temptations for its abuse. Some Methodist bishops use their power over ministerial appointments in an arbitrary and even ruthless way.

Prohibition and Abstinence

Another distinctive Methodist trait—which goes right back to John Wesley—is concern about social problems. Wesley devoted great energy to relieving the plight of the poor. He founded an unemployment bureau, organized a loan fund for small businessmen, conducted a charity school, and founded homes for orphans, widows, and the aged. He bitterly denounced greedy industrialists for exploiting workers, and organized boycotts to help break up the slave trade. He was particularly opposed to liquor and gambling, because he saw at first hand how much suffering they caused among poor families.

Methodists have continued to fight these battles into our own day. A denomination of doers, they have furnished the leadership for many civic drives, including those that resulted in regulating child labor and granting suffrage to women.

Of all the causes to which Methodists have rallied over the years, none has a greater emotional voltage than prohibition. The W.C.T.U. and the Anti-Saloon League were formed under Methodist leadership. That hatchet-swinging wrecker of barrooms Carry Nation was a good Methodist. The Eighteenth Amendment could never have been written into the Constitution without the fervent backing of thousands of Methodist ministers.

Since the repeal of national prohibition, the Methodist Board of Temperance has concentrated on trying to dry up one city or county at a time through local-option elections. The Methodist Church remains officially committed to total abstinence as the only Christian attitude toward alcohol.

This is what Methodists say officially through the pronouncements adopted at the General Conference—and there is no prospect of an early change. But it has been increasingly evident in recent years that a large number of Methodist laymen no longer believe in, or practice, total abstinence from liquor. Surveys conducted by the Church itself in various cities indicate that at least one third, and perhaps more than half, of the nation's Methodists see no harm in moderate drinking.

Another thing for which Methodists—and indeed all Protestants—are deeply indebted to John Wesley is the tradition of congregational singing. Wesley loved hymns and he thought they should be sung lustily by all worshipers, not by the choir only. Finding a dearth of hymns suitable for untrained voices, he asked his younger brother Charles to write a few. Charles Wesley obliged with more than six thousand hymns, many of which are still treasured by Protestants of every denomination.

"Think and Let Think"

Along with many good things, John Wesley bequeathed to his followers an indifferent attitude toward theology. "In opinions that do not strike at the root of Christianity, we Methodists think and let think," he said. Methodism has followed Wesley's lead by displaying great tolerance in matters of doctrine. In fact, the Methodist Church tolerates today, in many of its ministers, viewpoints that even the open-minded Wesley might consider to "strike at the root of Christianity." Surveys among Methodist clergy regularly turn up a fairly substantial percentage who regard Jesus simply as a great human teacher, and who deny the Incarnation, the Resurrection, and other central doctrines of the Apostles' Creed.

In fairness, it should be added that the Methodist Church has also produced men like Dr. Ralph Sockman and Dr. Edward W. Baumann, who are among the most articulate exponents of classic Christianity in the modern world.

With no clear doctrinal standards and no tradition of serious theological inquiry, Methodism has been peculiarly vulnerable to a danger that besets all churches in our day: the danger of substituting a sort of American folk religion for authentic Christianity. The components of this folk religion include a spirit of national loyalty to the "American way of life," and a belief that God stands ready, as a sort of cosmic errand boy, to provide peace of mind, success in business, health, and welfare for good church-going Americans who condescend to address Him in prayer. One subvariety of folk religion, which is quite popular among the Methodist laity, holds that it doesn't matter what a man believes so long as he "lives right"—the latter being defined in terms of whatever the particular speaker happens to regard as of particular importance, whether it be fighting for racial equality, abstaining from alcohol, or being nice to one's mother.

A Middle-class Denomination

For more than a century after it was formally established as a separate denomination (in 1784), American Methodism remained the "poor man's church," appealing primarily to the uneducated and underprivileged. But two long-term trends were changing Methodism. One was the disappearance of the frontier, which had done so much to shape early Methodist ways. The other was the steady rise in the educational level of the American people—a rise to which the Methodists themselves made an enormous contribution through the establishment of more than one hundred colleges and universities.*

These long-term trends, coupled with the increasing urbanization of American life and the general rise in living standards, gradually turned the Methodist Church into a middle-class denomination. Today it has more business and professional men than farmers and laborers. Other groups, such as the Pentecostal sects, which we'll consider in the next chapter, have taken over Methodism's historic role as the church of the poor.

* I record this Methodist contribution to American society with a sense of personal gratitude, since I was graduated from a great Methodist institution, Duke University.

As it has become wealthier and more respectable, the Methodist Church has lost much of its one-time zeal for evangelism. At the 1964 Methodist General Conference, the Board of Evangelism warned bluntly that the denomination's growth rate has been declining steadily for twelve years, and is now down to less than 1 per cent a year. Since the U.S. population is growing at a rate of 1.6 per cent a year, that means that each year the Methodist Church is composed of a slightly smaller proportion of the American people. Several years ago, the Southern Baptist Convention edged the Methodist Church out of the place it had long and proudly occupied as the nation's largest Protestant body.

Even as the second biggest Protestant denomination, however, the Methodist Church remains quite an impressive institution, with 40,000 local congregations, and upwards of 10.3 million members.

In addition to the major denomination, whose official title is The Methodist Church, there are twenty other Methodist bodies in the United States. Three of them are Negro denominations: the African Methodist Episcopal Church, the African Methodist Episcopal Zion Church, and the Christian Methodist Episcopal Church. Together they have about 2.5 million members. They have no important differences, and have been engaged since early 1964 in talks that may lead to a merger. The other Methodist bodies are small, ranging in size from the Free Methodist Church with 55,000 members to the Cumberland Methodist Church, which has fewer than 100 still in its fold. Most of these smaller bodies are Fundamentalist in doctrine.

SOCIETY OF FRIENDS

In an era when churches count their membership in millions, the Society of Friends, popularly known as Quakers, is a constant reminder that great size and great influence do not necessarily go hand in hand.

With fewer than 130,000 members in the United States, and about 60,000 in other countries, it is one of the world's smallest denominations. But it has left an indelible imprint on history, and it continues to enjoy a degree of public respect that many larger bodies envy.

Like the Congregationalists, Baptists, and Methodists, the Quakers are descended from that prolific mother communion, the Church of England.

George Fox's Inner Light

The founder of the Society of Friends was George Fox, who was born in 1624, the son of a weaver in Leicestershire, England. He was apprenticed to a cobbler to learn the shoemaker's trade, but Fox was more interested in souls than in soles. At the age of nineteen, he left home on an aimless pilgrimage, and spent the next four years wandering around England in search of a faith he could live by. He had a great distaste for the rituals and sacraments of the Established Church, which he regarded as empty formalism. One day, after much agonized seeking, Fox found himself "illuminated" by a great conviction that he did not need to search for God, because God was already present within him, "as close as breathing, as near as one's own limbs."

Out of this conviction, Fox developed the doctrine of the Inner Light which lies at the heart of the Quaker faith. It holds that God is ever present within every human being, and that He can be approached and experienced directly by anyone who sincerely seeks Him. This is, of course, a form of mysticism—but it is a simple and practical kind of mysticism, as suitable for ordinary people as for cloistered saints.

There is no official Quaker creed, and once you get past the doctrine of the Inner Light it is difficult to make any blanket statements about what Quakers believe. Most of them see in Jesus Christ the supreme revelation of God's nearness to and love for all men. But no Friend is required to accept any particular theological definition of Christ's person or mission. As the famed Quaker writer Rufus Jones has put it, "Friends are not much interested in abstract theories and statements about God. They prefer to begin with personal experience of Him."

Quakers have drawn several corollaries from the doctrine of the Inner Light. One man's opinion—on a religious question or any other topic—is as good as another's. Every human being, however poor and lowly, possesses vast dignity and importance, because he bears within him the divine spark. No outward ritual or sacrament is necessary for men to draw nigh to God. Baptism is not a rite using water, but an inner baptism of the spirit. Holy Communion is not to be celebrated with consecrated bread and wine, but in silent spiritual union with God.

The Persecuted Friends

These doctrines were considered extremely radical when they were first put forward by Fox, who took up a career as an itinerant preacher in order to expound them. The small bands of "Friends" who gathered around him were subjected to harsh persecution by church and civil authorities. Their troubles mounted when Fox decided that it was wrong to show obeisance to anyone but God—and forbade his followers to doff their hats to the King. At one point, in the middle of the seventeenth century, there were four thousand Quakers in England's jails, At least four hundred died as martyrs to their convictions.

The name "Quaker" resulted from one of Fox's frequent trips before trial magistrates (he was sentenced to prison six times). Instead of pleading for the court's mercy, Fox sternly adjured the judge to "tremble with fear of the Lord." The judge turned the advice back on Fox, and called him a "quaker."

Quakers began emigrating to America soon after the Puritan colony was established in Massachusetts. But they encountered as harsh treatment on this side of the Atlantic as on the other. On the State House lawn in Boston you can see the statue of Mary Dyer, a woman whom the Puritans put to death for refusing to recant her Quaker beliefs. There were many like her, to whom no statues have been raised. The Quakers endured, and by 1672, when George Fox paid a visit to America, there were small Quaker settlements all along the coast, with particularly sizable concentrations in Maryland and Rhode Island—the only two colonies that granted religious freedom to Quakers.

One of the English Quakers, William Penn, was the son of a wealthy nobleman. Through his father's influence at court, he obtained the King's consent for establishment of a Quaker colony in America. Penn arrived in 1682 and founded the "City of Brotherly Love," Philadelphia, and the colony of Pennsylvania.

The colonial Quakers, in Pennsylvania and elsewhere, were hard-working, thrifty, rigorously honest people. Their settlements invariably prospered. But the Quakers never grew greatly in number. Following Fox's lead, they strove for simplicity of life, and carried this quest to the extreme of using "plain" language ("thee" and "thou") and wearing "plain" clothing (the simple black garb familiar to anyone who has seen it pictured on the Quaker Oats package). They also forbade drinking, dancing, and other "worldly amusements." Inevitably, they became identified as a "peculiar people"—a reputation which at once discouraged converts and led to defections among their own young people.

Turning the Other Cheek

The tendency of the American Friends to develop a ghetto mentality was heightened during the Revolution. Fox taught that war was the very antithesis of the Christian spirit, and strictly forbade his followers to bear arms under any circumstances. Indeed, the Friends took literally Christ's teaching that one should turn the other cheek when struck. Refusing to return violence, or even to resist it, they were sitting pigeons for the mobs of bullies who ranged through Philadelphia and other Quaker communities during the Revolution, seeking "nonpatriots" who had failed to support the war.

Pacifism has continued to be a distinctive Quaker "witness." But many Quakers today feel that pacifism is an ideal that cannot practically be attained in a world where Communists and other aggressors are ever ready to pounce on the defenseless. Thousands of Quaker youth have served in uniform during and since World War II, and it is by no means uncommon to encounter today a Quaker, like former Vice President Richard M. Nixon, who is an outspoken advocate of powerful national defenses.

Quaker concern for humanity has been expressed in many ways besides pacifism. A century ago, Quakers were working tirelessly for the abolition of slavery; today they are working with equal fervor to eliminate the remaining vestiges of racial discrimination. Through their American Friends Service Committee, Quakers are at work in a score of countries around the world, feeding the hungry, clothing the naked, sheltering the orphans, treating the sick.

Despite their avoidance of formal creeds, Quakers have not been immune to the devisive effects of doctrinal disputes that have plagued other Christian bodies. Because of a difference of opinion that dates back to 1827, American Quakers today are split into two major groups. The largest, with about 70,000 members, is the Five Years Meeting of Friends. The Religious Society of Friends General Conference has about 30,000 members. There are several smaller groups not affiliated with either of the national organizations.

Some Quaker congregations employ salaried pastors and conduct "programmed" worship services that are similar to those of other Protestant churches. Many of these so-called "pastoral" groups are in the Five Years Meeting.

The original Quaker practice, still maintained in a majority of the General Conference congregations, calls for no pastor, and no formal program of worship. The congregation assembles on "First day" (Sunday) in its severely unadorned, altarless meetinghouse "on the basis of silence." Out of their silent waiting may come a Bible quotation, vocal prayer, a brief testimony or message—from any member who feels "called" to participate.

After about an hour of worship, the meeting ends with each Friend shaking hands with his neighbor.

THE MENNONITES

It is easy to confuse Mennonites and Quakers, as people demonstrate almost daily to the great distress of members of both these venerable religious bodies. They have a number of points of similarity, including a commitment to pacifism, an insistence on simplicity of life—and a strong tendency to live in Pennsylvania.

But the Mennonites emphatically are *not* an offshoot of the Friends movement. Actually, they deserve to be listed as one of the original Reformation churches—along with the Lutherans, Presbyterians, and Anglicans. For they are the direct spiritual descendants of the Anabaptist movement, which was founded in Zurich, Switzerland, in 1535 by the Swiss reformer Ulrich Zwingli, and quickly spread to the Netherlands and Germany.

The Anabaptists have been called "the left wing of the Reformation" because they went much further than Luther or Calvin in repudiating the doctrines of the Roman Catholic Church and in trying to return to the "original Christianity" that they found in the New Testament.

Among other things, the Anabaptists rejected the whole idea of infant baptism, and insisted that only an adult believer could be validly baptized. The name Anabaptist means "rebaptizer," reflecting their practice of administering baptism anew to adults who had been baptized as infants.

No religious body has ever been subjected to a more relentless and bloody persecution than the Anabaptists. They were persecuted by Catholics, by Lutherans, and by Calvinists with equal zeal. They were hanged, burned at the stake, and drowned—a form of death which Swiss Calvinists considered very appropriate for persons who held "heretical" views about baptism. Within a period of ten years, more than five thousand Anabaptists were martyred in Europe.

Some of the survivors fled to North Germany, under the leadership of a former Roman Catholic priest named Menno Simons; hence, they became known as "Mennonites." They ultimately moved from Germany into Central Europe, where they settled on wastelands that no one else wanted, and brought them into fruitful cultivation through their great skill as farmers.

In 1683 a group of Mennonites from Central Europe found a haven of tolerance in Quaker Pennsylvania. Others soon followed. Within a few years there was a steady flow of Mennonite immigrants to free America. Today, nearly half of the world's 500,000 Mennonites live in the United States. Pennsylvania remains their main center of strength, but there also are large groups in Indiana, Ohio, Kansas, Michigan, and the Dakotas, and smaller bodies in nearly every other state.

Although all Mennonites share the same basic heritage, they differ on details. There are about twenty distinct groupings within the Mennonite family.

The Amish and the Hutterian Brethren

One of the most colorful and widely publicized is the Old Order Amish Colony of Pennsylvania, whose 18,000 members refuse to ride in automobiles, wear hooks and eyes instead of buttons on their coats, and in other ways seek to perpetuate ancient folkways.

Another relatively small branch which attracts a lot of public attention because of its "peculiar" ways is the Hutterian Brethren, about 12,000 of whom live in isolated agricultural colonies in the Midwest, where they practice common ownership of property.

The largest number of Mennonites—about 80,000—belong to a denomination known as The Mennonite Church. Next largest is The General Conference Mennonite Church, with about 52,000 members.

In both these bodies, the men are clean-shaven and wear ordinary business suits. The women dress modestly, without make-up or jewelry, but rarely are seen in "quaint" costumes.

Mennonite worship is simple and austere, built around

the exposition of texts from the Bible, which is interpreted literally as the "inspired, inerrant, authoritative" Word of God. Church membership is never a mere social convention, but is taken very seriously as a pledge of commitment to Christian discipleship. Those who willfully disobey Christ's teachings, as the Mennonites understand them, are liable to expulsion from the fellowship.

Mennonites disapprove of drinking, smoking, dancing, card-playing and movies. But these prohibitions are regarded as incidental bulwarks of a holy life. The main Mennonite emphasis is not to be found in any "shalt not" but in one mighty "shalt"—"Thou shalt love the Lord thy God with all thy heart . . . and thy neighbor as thyself."

Mennonites contend that Christ meant exactly what he said when he told his disciples to love their enemies, to turn the other cheek, to offer no resistance to those who would do them evil. They believe that any use of force— and particularly the waging of war—is totally incompatible with this commandment. So they are uncompromising pacifists, refusing not only to bear arms, but also to hold office as magistrates or policemen.

If you tell a Mennonite that this is unrealistic, and that it opens the way for the strong to exploit the weak, and for the wicked to enslave the good, he will not try to argue with you. He will simply tell you that Mennonites are determined to take the Lord's words at their face value, regardless of what it may cost. And he will remind you that Jesus told his disciples they should expect to suffer for his sake.

CHAPTER VIII

The Faiths Born in America

In addition to the churches that were transplanted from Europe, America has eight thriving religious movements that are native to its own soil. They differ enormously in size, polity, and doctrine. In fact, the only thing they have in common is that they were born in America. Some are Protestant bodies. Others, while bearing traces of the Protestant culture from which they emerged, have moved so far from orthodoxy that they cannot be described as Christian without giving to that term a latitude that deprives it of all meaning.

THE CHRISTIANS

Oldest and largest of the religious movements indigenous to the United States is a fellowship whose members reject all denominational labels and call themselves simply "Christians."

There are two main branches of this movement. One has about 8000 local congregations, with 1.8 million members. Each congregation enjoys complete autonomy in managing its affairs, but there is a national convention which meets once a year, and a national secretariat with offices at Indianapolis, Indiana, to provide some degree of organizational cohesion. This body is known as The International Convention of Christian Churches (Disciples of Christ) and its members are known informally as Disciples.

The other branch comprises about 10,000 local congregations, with an estimated 2 million members. Each local congregation is termed a Church of Christ, and the movement as a whole bears the name Churches of Christ. But it is even more loosely knit than the Disciples of Christ, having no national convention and no central offices or agencies of any kind. The nearest thing to a national meeting is a Lectureship held each year by Abilene Christian College, Abilene, Texas, which draws thousands of Churches of Christ leaders from various sections of the country for five days of informal consultation and fellowship.

Both the Disciples and the Churches of Christ are represented in all fifty states. Disciples' strength is greatest in the South and the Midwest. Churches of Christ are concentrated in Texas, Arkansas, Louisiana, Tennessee, Mississippi, Alabama, and Georgia.

The Partiarchs of the Movement

Patriarch of the movement was a frontier preacher named Barton W. Stone, who was born in Maryland in 1772. He was an ordained Presbyterian clergyman when he went to the frontier to begin his career as a conductor of revival meetings. But he soon became convinced that denominationalism is the curse of Christianity. In 1804, he issued a manifesto, repudiating all the denominational labels and "man-made creeds" that divide Christians. He called upon believers in the Bible to unite in a new fellowship, based solely upon the teachings of Scripture. He suggested that they call themselves "Christians" to make it clear that they were not any particular brand or denomination of Christians.

In his impatience with denominationalism and disunity, Barton Stone was one hundred and fifty years ahead of the ecumenical spirit that pervades today's churches. But even in the early nineteenth century, he found plenty of people who shared his sentiments. The Christian movement gained adherents rapidly, especially in the frontier communities of Kentucky, Tennessee, and Missouri.

It got a tremendous impetus after 1809 from the leadership of a remarkable father-and-son team, Thomas and Alexander Campbell. The Campbells were Irish Presbyterians, who immigrated to America and became frontier evangelists. Like Barton Stone, they were passionately convinced that all Christians should unite—not in a hierarchical church but in a voluntary fellowship based on the sole authority of the Bible and the absolute independence of each local congregation.

Alexander Campbell was a formidable preacher who won the admiration of intellectuals like James Madison as well as the enthusiastic response of frontier tent-meeting crowds. In an era when Protestant and Catholic contacts were virtually nil, he cultivated a close friendship with the

Catholic Archbishop of Cincinnati, the Most Reverend John Purcell, and once engaged in a public debate with him.

No Creed but Christ

The Christian movement carried to its logical conclusion the Protestant principle that each man is free to read and interpret the Scriptures for himself. "No creed but Christ" is a slogan dear to the heart of every Christian. In practice, it means that any person who accepts Jesus Christ as his personal Lord and Saviour is welcome as a member of the fellowship, without any further doctrinal tests or standards.

This "creedlessness" does not lead to as much doctrinal anarchy as an outsider might suspect, however. For belief in the Bible is an equally cardinal tenet of the movement. Some Christians take the Bible literally; others are quite liberal in their approach; but all take it seriously as the one and only yardstick of doctrine. This attitude also has been enshrined in a popular Christian slogan: "Where the Scriptures speak, we speak; where the Scriptures are silent, we are silent."

Even this slogan, however, is subject to various interpretations. Does it mean that modern churches are to eschew practices that are not explicitly mentioned in the Bible—such as the use of organs and other instrumental music, or the formation of missionary societies? The more conservative Christians believe that it does mean this. The more liberal ones believe that churches are free to do things that are in the spirit of the New Testament, or that can reasonably be inferred from the practices of the primitive church.

The Rift in the Movement

This question caused a rift in the Christian movement after 1906, and led to the present existence of two entirely separate branches, which have relatively little to do with one another.

Both the Disciples and the Churches of Christ resemble the Baptists in practicing baptism by immersion and in restricting the rite to those mature enough to make a personal decision of faith in Christ. Both also have the distinctive custom of celebrating the Lord's Supper every Sunday. Christians feel that these two practices are warranted by Scripture.

Churches of Christ still forbid all instrumental music. And they do not have missionary societies. Each missionary is supported by an individual congregation. A minister is referred to as Elder Jones or Mr. Jones, but *never* the Reverend John Jones. Use of the title Reverend is considered very unscriptural.

Disciples of Christ have organs in their churches, and have evolved not only missionary societies, but most of the other organizational trappings of a typical American Protestant denomination. Unlike the Churches of Christ, whose fear of ecclesiastical organization causes them to keep aloof from ecumenical bodies, the Disciples have played a major role in the National Council of Churches. They also were charter members of the Consultation on Church Union, which was formed in 1961 to explore the possibility of a six-way merger of leading American Protestant bodies.

Thus the Disciples are continuing to display—in a modern context—the devotion to the cause of Christian unity that brought the movement into being.

UNITARIANS AND UNIVERSALISTS

The Unitarian Universalist Association was formed in 1961 by the merger of two denominations that originated in New England in the early nineteenth century.

The word *Unitarian* (from the Latin, *unus*) originally signified a rejection of the orthodox trinitarian concept of God as three Persons—Father, Son, and Holy Spirit—united in one Godhead. The unitarian view was expounded as early as the fourth century by Arius of Alexandria, who taught that Jesus was sent from God, but was not actually God incarnate. This doctrine was branded a heresy in A.D. 325 by the Council of Nicea, which asserted in the Nicene Creed (still adhered to by a large majority of the world's Christians) that Jesus was "very God of very God . . . being of one substance with the Father."

Unitarian views continued to bob up over the centuries. A Spaniard, Michael Servetus, was burned at the stake in Calvin's Geneva in 1535 for teaching "unitarian heresies." During the eighteenth century, a number of English and European intellectuals embraced a unitarian philosophy.

The New England Unitarianism

It was in America, however, that the Unitarian movement first emerged as an organized denomination. It flowered in New England after 1819 under the leadership of William

Ellery Channing, Ralph Waldo Emerson, and Theodore Parker.

For a time, Unitarianism threatened to engulf the long-established Congregational churches of New England. Within a few years, one hundred twenty-five of New England's leading Congregational churches, including twenty of the oldest in America, turned Unitarian. Thomas Jefferson, who was greatly attracted to the new movement, predicted that within a generation every American would be a Unitarian.

This forecast proved to be very wide of the mark. The Unitarian Association never grew larger than 200,000 members. But it enjoyed a prestige far exceeding its size because among its members were such men as John Adams, John Quincy Adams, Daniel Webster, John Marshall, Oliver Wendell Holmes, Henry David Thoreau, and John Greenleaf Whittier.

The early Unitarians considered themselves to be Christians because, even though they did not regard Jesus as divine, they did look upon him as one sent by God to lead men into the way, the truth, and the life.

But the Christian orientation of the Unitarian movement diminished steadily through the years. From the start, Unitarians placed great emphasis on individual freedom of belief. Revolting against the Calvinist tendency to spell everything out in rigid orthodoxies, the Unitarians refused to have any creed, any dogmas, or any definitions of faith. They left each member free to "seek the truth for himself," and to believe only what he personally found to be reasonable and logically persuasive.

Today there are still "conservative" Unitarians—especially in New England—who revere Jesus as the greatest of all teachers, and who try to emulate his life and follow his teachings as they appear in the New Testament. But there are many other Unitarians who do not attach any more value to the teachings of Jesus than to those of Buddha or Abraham Lincoln, and who feel that the Hindu Vedas, the Hebrew Talmud, and the writings of Earl Russell are as good a source of inspiration as the Gospels. There are, indeed, a substantial number of Unitarian ministers and laymen who do not subscribe to the concept of a personal God, and who are indistinguishable in their beliefs from atheistic humanists.

The Evolution of Universalism

Universalism has gone through a similar evolution. It started as a religious movement animated by one distinctive conviction: that all men would be saved. From this doctrine of universal salvation, it progressed by degrees to a denial of the divinity of Christ, and a rejection of other orthodox Christian doctrines.

The first Universalist congregation was established in Gloucester, Massachusetts, in 1779 by a former Wesleyan minister named John Murray. It gained adherents rapidly among people who were reacting against the harsh Calvinist doctrine of predestination. By 1790, there were enough Universalist churches to establish a national association. But the new denomination failed to maintain its early growth rate. By the time of its merger with the Unitarians in 1961, the Universalist Church claimed only about 70,000 members.

The charter of the Unitarian Universalist Association refrains from mentioning the name of Jesus. It proclaims the purpose of the Association: "to cherish and spread the universal truths taught by the great prophets and teachers of humanity in every age and tradition, immemorially summarized in the Judaeo-Christian heritage as love to God and love to man."

It says that members of the Association have come together in religious fellowship in order "to strengthen one another in a free and disciplined search for truth" and "to affirm, defend and promote the supreme worth of every human personality, the dignity of man, and the use of the democratic method in human relationships." Another purpose of the Association is "to implement our vision of one world by striving for a world community founded on ideals of brotherhood, justice and peace."

As these articles indicate, Unitarian Universalists tend to be liberals not only in theology, but in their attitude toward public affairs. No religious denomination has been more outspoken in combating social injustice and in working for a stable world peace.

Preoccupation with Social Problems

The preoccupation of Unitarian Universalist churches with social problems is reflected in their worship services, which usually feature topical sermons that are really lectures on current events rather than expositions of Bible texts.

Although they do not regard baptism and Holy Communion as sacraments, they recognize that these traditional Christian rites may have sentimental associations for some people; they therefore provide for what might be called de-natured observances. In lieu of baptism, for example, some Unitarian Universalist churches have a "child dedication ceremony" in which water is used as "a symbol of purity."

As a substitute for communion, some churches conduct a service in which each member brings his favorite flower. The different kinds of flowers represent the individuality and uniqueness of each human personality. They are gathered into bouquets to represent the bonds of unity among mankind. Upon leaving, each person takes another type flower with him. This indicates that "in intercommunion with each other we give and receive, not always knowing to whom we give or from whom we receive."

THE MORMONS

Mormons are the products, and in some sense the prisoners, of a unique history.

Their history begins with a farm boy named Joseph Smith, Jr., who lived near the village of Palmyra, New York, in the early nineteenth century. He was strongly affected by revival meetings, to which his mother took him, but he did not join a church because he was confused by the great variety of doctrines that were being stridently proclaimed by the various Protestant denominations as they jostled for converts in frontier communities.

In 1820, when he was fourteen years old, Joseph Smith began to spend much time alone in the woods near his home, experiencing what he later described as a series of religious visions. In these visions, he said, he was visited by an angel named Moroni, who finally directed him to a secret cache in a hillside where he found a box full of golden plates inscribed with strange hieroglyphics. Moroni also provided a pair of "instruments"—called Urim and Thummin—to enable the barely literate farm lad to understand the writing on the golden plates, and to dictate an English translation to a local schoolmaster. The result, published in 1829, was the famous Book of Mormon (a name which Smith said was a compound of English and Egyptian, and which he translated as "more good").

The Book of Mormon tells the story of a lost tribe of Israelites who migrated to America about 600 B.C. and who became the ancestors of the American Indians. After his resurrection, Christ came to America to visit these people, and to establish his church among them. The members of the original church were wiped out in a tribal war in A.D. 385, but the last survivor, Moroni, managed before his death to hide the golden plates on which their history was recorded. The book ends with a prophecy that the true church of Christ would someday be restored in America by a group of "latter-day saints," who would correct the doctrinal errors of the other churches and restore the communal life of the New Testament Christians.

The Book of Mormon caused a sensation along the frontier, and Smith soon found himself with a fairly large body of disciples and a much larger body of enemies. His disciples called him "the Prophet" and themselves "the Latter-day Saints."* In 1831 Smith established the first Mor-

* The official name of the principal Mormon body is still The Church of Jesus Christ of Latter-day Saints. But outsiders have always called it The Mormon Church, and in recent years Mormons have bowed to the inevitable and accepted this synonym.

mon community at Kirtland, Ohio. It began with one
hundred fifty settlers and quickly grew to more than one
thousand. In the same year, Smith visited Jackson County,
Missouri, and founded a Mormon community near the
present site of Independence, Missouri.

The Persecuted

Pastors and members of old-line Protestant churches looked
upon the new movement with horror. They held the Bible
in great reverence, and felt that Smith and his followers
were committing the worst kind of blasphemy in depicting
the Book of Mormon as an addition to the Holy Scriptures.
Persecution of the Mormons began almost immediately.
Within a few years they had been driven out of Missouri
by armed vigilantes, aided in some instances by the state
militia. The refugees from Missouri joined forces with
Smith's following from Ohio to found a town named Nauvoo in Illinois. Smith was its mayor as well as its spiritual
leader, and it quickly grew into a larger and thriving city.
But public hostility toward the Mormons was further in-
flamed by reports that polygamy was being practiced in
Nauvoo; in 1844 the governor of Illinois sent the militia
into Nauvoo. Smith was arrested, and taken to the nearby
city of Carthage, where the militia permitted a mob to
storm the jail and lynch him on June 27, 1844.
     The mantle of the martyred Prophet passed to Brigham
Young, a Vermont house-painter who proved to be one of
the greatest leaders ever produced on the American fron-

tier. Young decided that the only way Mormons could avoid persecution was to go to a land so bleak and unpromising that no one else would want it. He found what he was looking for in the valley of the Great Salt Lake in Utah (then a part of Mexico), and in 1847 he led the first Mormon pioneers on the grueling overland trek to Utah. Thousands of Mormon families followed during the next thirty years, suffering incredible hardships. Many walked every foot of the way, pushing their meager belongings in handcarts. Hundreds died along the way, and hundreds more did not survive the first winter of settlement in as harsh and inhospitable an environment as was ever selected for colonization.

Merely to have survived the rigors of their new home would be a tribute to the hardiness of the Mormon pioneers. But they did more than survive. Bearing one another's burdens in a close bond of community fellowship, and fired with the zealous faith that persecution always seems to produce, the Mormons turned the Utah desert into one of the most fertile and prosperous lands on earth. It is fashionable today for outsiders to raise eyebrows at the vast wealth of the Mormon Church—and it is one of the richest institutions in the world, with huge holdings in agriculture, mining, transportation, real estate, and other industries—but it should never be forgotten that the Mormons made their fortune the hard way. And if much of the community's wealth was held in the name of the Church, that was a natural result of a historical situation in which the Church was the center of business, educational, and social as well as religious life.

The Polygamy Issue

But moving to Utah did not end the Mormons' persecution. After the Mexican War in 1848, Utah became a United States territory. At first the federal government left the Mormons to manage their own affairs, with Young as territorial governor. But the polygamy issue became a political football in the East, and to appease Protestants (who seem to be able to work up a greater pitch of fanaticism where sex is concerned than on any other subject) the government sent troops into Utah in 1857 to depose Young as governor. The Civil War gave the Mormons a respite from federal harassment. By 1887, however, the anti-Morman bigots were in business again, and Congress passed a law disenfranchising all Mormon votes and confiscating all church properties.

In 1890 the Mormons finally made peace with the Guardians of Morality in Washington by outlawing the teaching and practice of plural marriage. Restoration of church property and Mormon voting rights followed, and in 1896 Utah was finally admitted to the Union as a state.

It is a colorful history, and one that does great credit to Mormon courage and fidelity. It has left its imprint on the Mormons of today. You can see its influence, for example, in the storehouses which the Church maintains in easy reach of every Mormon community. There is enough food and clothing in these storehouses to take care of all members of the Church for more than a year, and no Mormon ever needs to turn to public welfare agencies in time of need. The strong bonds of fellowship forged during the years of common suffering also are reflected in the continuing clannishness of Mormon communities, and in the sacrifices that Mormons cheerfully make for their church. The zeal for their faith which was fanned by past persecutions is manifested today in the readiness of young Mormons to devote two years of their lives to missionary service, at their own expense.

But Mormons are also prisoners of their history, in the sense that they have inherited from Joseph Smith, and to a lesser degree from Brigham Young, a number of doctrines that set them apart from normative Christianity and stamp them in the minds of many as a peculiar sect.

Distinctive Mormon Doctrines

There is a strong tendency in modern Mormonism to soft-pedal these distinctive doctrines and to emphasize the articles of faith that Mormons hold in common with main-line Protestant bodies. In fact, you could attend a Mormon Sunday school for weeks in a row without hearing any teaching that would be recognizably different from that which you might encounter in a Fundamentalist Protestant church.

But the Mormon distinctives are still there—in the Book of Mormon and other writings which are officially held to be based on divine revelation—and there seems to be no way in which the Mormons can escape them without repudiating their own history, which they are not about to do.

One of these distinctive Mormon teachings—which has lately been a source of great embarrassment to such Mormon politicians as George Romney—is that all human beings have an unremembered pre-existence in the spirit world. The black skins with which Negroes are born is a sign of divine displeasure with their conduct in that prior life. Thus, Negroes are forbidden to enter the Mormon priesthood, which is otherwise open to all males.

Mormon views about God and Jesus Christ are hard for an outsider to fathom. Much Mormon literature and preaching today seems to say substantially what Protestants and Catholics say. But one can also find in Smith's writings and other Mormon literature the concept that God is a flesh-and-bones person, who became supreme by mastering universal knowledge. Jesus, in these writings, is depicted as God's son, but only in the sense of being the first of many children to go through a phase of incarnation after a long prior existence in the spirit world. Mormon doctrine holds that all human beings who live worthily in this stage of their existence can look forward to a future life in the ex-alted status of sons or daughters of God. And this future life will be a bodily one, which will include marriage and the procreation of children. Indeed, to be married and beget children is in Mormon belief one of the essential condi-tions of celestial bliss. That is why there was great social pressure for plural marriages in a society where women outnumbered men. To a Mormon woman, a polygamous marriage was infinitely preferable to entering heaven with-out a husband.

Because the link between Mormons and polygamy is so strong in many minds, it should be emphasized that only a very small percentage of the Utah families ever practiced plural marriage; their motives were religious conviction, not sexual lust; and polygamy has been strictly outlawed for the best part of a century. Moreover, polygamy was *never* condoned by one substantial branch of the Mormon family, which did not join the trek to Utah but continued to live in the East, with its center at Independence, Missouri. This branch is called The Reorganized Church of Latter-day Saints and it now has about 160,000 members. (It also rejects the teaching that Negroes are under a divine curse.)

The main LDS church, which has its world headquarters in Salt Lake City, has 1.8 million members in the United States, and about 500,000 more in England, Western Europe, Australia, and other overseas areas where Mormons are conducting vigorous missionary work.

The LDS church has no professional clergy as such. Every Mormon boy is eligible for ordination to the priesthood at about the same age that he would be confirmed in another church. Local congregations are called "wards" and the man who serves as pastor is known as a bishop. He is usually a business or professional man who handles his pastoral duties on a part-time basis, without salary. At the head of the Mormon hierarchy is the Council of the Twelve Apostles and the President of the Church, who is regarded as a divinely guided prophet.

Mormons observe strict rules of personal morality. They do not approve of tea, coffee, tobacco, or alcohol. They disapprove of birth control, and divorce is unthinkable, especially if the couple have been united in a Mormon temple ceremony (the only kind that is considered capable of cementing a celestial marriage that will endure into the next life). Mormon churches provide the most extensive and best-organized youth programs of any denomination, hands down and no contest.

SEVENTH-DAY ADVENTISTS

Seventh-day Adventists are Christians in a hurry. They believe that the Second Coming of Christ is imminent. So they feel a strong sense of urgency about getting on with the Lord's work—particularly in fulfilling his command to preach the gospel to every nation.

The first Adventist missionary, John Nevins Andrews, was sent out (to John Calvin's Switzerland, for some strange reason) in 1874. Today there are Adventist missionaries at work in 189 of the world's 223 nations. Although the denomination has only about 300,000 members in the United States—its home base—it has at least three times that many in its foreign missions.

The far-flung Adventist missionary program—which totally eclipses the efforts of many large Protestant denominations—is carried on by an efficient, highly structured world-wide organization, which is made up of more than 6000 ordained ministers and some 50,000 other full-time salaried workers, including doctors, nurses, teachers, and technicians. Adventists operate more than 5000 schools, nearly 300 hospitals and clinics, and 44 publishing houses that turn out religious literature in more than 200 languages.

The Most Generous Fundamentalists

Adventists finance this massive global enterprise by giving more generously to their church than do the members of any other large denomination. Virtually all Adventists tithe, and many give a "double tithe"—20 per cent of their income. When the National Council of Churches publishes its annual report on contributions, the per capita figure for Seventh-day Adventists is always about five times the average of all Protestant denominations.

Adventists belong to the Fundamentalist wing of Protestantism, which believes in literal interpretation of the Bible. In fact, they go beyond many other Fundamentalists in regarding the laws and prophecies of the Old Testament as being as fully applicable to modern Christians as are the teachings of the New Testament. That is why they observe the seventh day of the week—the traditional Jewish Sabbath, from sundown Friday to sundown Saturday—as a day of worship, instead of the Christian Sunday.

Their reading of biblical prophecies, especially those found in the apocalyptic books of Daniel and Revelation (Apocalypse), convinces them that the time is near for Christ to return to earth in the promised "Second Advent." Exactly how near, they do not profess to know. The Church strictly forbids any attempt to set a specific year or date.

The Second Advent and Emphasis on Health

This rule is deeply rooted in Adventist history. Early in the nineteenth century, in this country and in Europe, a movement developed spontaneously around the belief that the Second Coming of Christ was at hand. Its adherents were first called "Millerites," after one of their leaders, William Miller, who predicted that the Day of Judgment would fall between March 21, 1843, and

March 21, 1844. Thousands of believers sold their property, gave away all their money, and waited prayerfully for the event. When the deadline came and passed, most of these early Adventists abandoned the movement in disillusionment.

But a small group in the New England states remained convinced that the Second Advent was likely to come at any time, even though the precise day and hour could not be reckoned. This group included a remarkable woman named Ellen White, who wrote scores of books and hundreds of articles and pamphlets that set the theological tone of Seventh-day Adventism.

The Church was formally organized in 1863 at Battle Creek, Michigan. It had an initial membership of about 3500.

Mrs. White was a strong advocate of good health, and this emphasis has become part of the Adventist heritage. The first Adventist medical institution was the famed Battle Creek Sanitarium. The denomination now operates excellent hospitals, sanitariums, and clinics around the world.

Adventists are forbidden, on grounds of health, to use alcohol, tobacco, tea, or coffee. They are urged to stick to a simple vegetarian diet, avoiding meats, hot spices, and rich desserts. But vegetarianism is not a "test" of membership.

The Church also frowns on movies and dancing, which it regards as unwholesome influences on young people. Adventist girls may use cosmetics in moderation, but they are advised that jewelry is "a display of pride and vanity" and a waste of money that should be used in the work of the Kingdom.

Although their hopes are vividly fixed on another world, Adventists take very seriously Jesus' example of ministering to human suffering in this one. In addition to their globe-circling network of medical institutions, they carry on one of the largest welfare programs ever undertaken by a private agency. Each year, more than 6 million indigent people receive food, clothing, or other help from Seventh-day Adventist welfare workers.

Adventist work around the world is directed from a General Conference headquarters in Washington, D.C. Local congregations are largely self-governing, but their pastors are appointed by regional conferences, composed of elected delegates from each church.

Adventist ministers are required to have completed five years of college and two years of internship before they are ordained. They are never called "Reverend" (Adventists believe that that term belongs only to God), but are known as "Elder" or "Pastor."

CHRISTIAN SCIENTISTS

One Thursday evening in February, 1866, a frail young widow named Mary Baker Eddy was seriously injured by a fall on an icy sidewalk in Lynn, Massachusetts.

She was carried unconscious to a nearby home. For two days she remained in critical condition and her friends despaired of her life. Sunday afternoon, Mrs. Eddy asked for a Bible. She read (in the ninth chapter of Matthew) the account of Christ's healing of a man bedridden with palsy.

Although she had read the familiar passage many times before, on this occasion Mrs. Eddy found in it a new significance. After a brief prayer, she closed the Bible, arose from bed, dressed herself, and walked into the parlor to greet her startled friends.

Out of this event, and Mrs. Eddy's subsequent reflections, grew one of America's major religious denominations—The Christian Science Church. Formally established in Boston in 1879, it now has more than 3200 branches in forty-eight countries. In keeping with Mrs. Eddy's wish, the Church does not publish membership statistics, but it is known to have several hundred thousand adherents.

Their Basic Philosophy

Christian Science is usually identified in the public mind with spiritual healing. But the Church's distinctive teachings about health can be understood only in the context of its basic theology, which is outlined in Mrs. Eddy's book *Science and Health, with Key to the Scriptures.*

Christian Scientists believe that God is "infinite good," and that all "reality" in the universe is necessarily good because God created it.

The evil, sickness, and death that men think they see in the world could not have come from God; hence, they must be essentially unreal. They afflict men only so long as erring human belief causes them to seem real. When men achieve true spiritual understanding, the "illusions" of sin and sickness vanish, just as a bad dream evaporates when the dreamer awakens.

Christian Scientists say that thousands of people have been healed of every kind of disease and ailment, from cancer to broken bones, by the application of this insight. They do not regard these healings as "miracles" but as the natural working of divine laws which are impartially available to all men.

It should be emphasized that, in Christian Science teaching, the "healing" that flows from apprehension of spiritual truth is not confined to physical illness, but also applies to family and business problems, social injustices, psychological tensions, and, most important of all, to moral weakness. "The emphatic purpose of Christian Science," Mrs. Eddy wrote, "is the healing of sin."

Although Christian Scientists acknowledge Jesus in their formal creed as the Son of God, their favorite term for him is "The Way-shower." They believe that Christ came to save men from a false material concept of existence, by demonstrating in his healing ministry and his resurrection "the allness of soul and spirit and the nothingness of matter."

The Christian Science Church has no ordained clergy. The healing ministry is entrusted to "practitioners," men and women who are licensed for this service after careful examination of their understanding of Christian Science doctrines.

In local churches, all of which are branches of the original "Mother Church" in Boston, Sunday worship services are conducted by "readers" elected by the congregation. Passages from the Bible and from Mrs. Eddy's *Science and Health* are read at every Sunday service. At midweek, usually on Wednesday evening, Christian Science churches conduct testimonial meetings at which persons healed of illness relate their experiences.

Most churches also sponsor one or more "Reading Rooms," at which any interested person may find extensive literature on Christian Science.

THE PENTECOSTALS

America's fast-growing Pentecostal movement is composed of more than twenty organized denominations plus uncounted thousands of independent local churches and storefront sects.

Their common bond is an intensely emotional approach to religion.

Pentecostals adhere to the characteristic doctrines of Protestant Fundamentalism, including the literal interpretation of the Bible. But they have an additional doctrine which is distinctively their own, and which is the hallmark of their movement: They believe that authentic religious conversion is an ecstatic experience, and should be accompanied by all the "signs" which attended the outpouring of God's Holy Spirit upon the first Christian Apostles.

The Gift of Tongues

The New Testament says that these signs included "the gift of tongues." On the first day of Pentecost, when the Apostles were filled with the Spirit, they found themselves able to speak and understand many strange languages that they had never learned.

Pentecostals say this phenomenon still occurs among believers who are stirred by genuine religious fervor. Other churches do not experience it, they say, because they have allowed "ecclesiastical formalism" to stifle the natural expression of religious emotions.

At their worship services, Pentecostals display their feelings in an uninhibited and often exuberant way. They shout, clap hands, sing, and march. Some may speak in tongues or fall to the floor in a trance. This has prompted some irreverent outsiders to apply to Pentecostals the derisive nickname "Holy Rollers."

The Pentecostal movement was an outgrowth of the popular religious revivals that swept the world during the latter part of the nineteenth century. Although there are some Pentecostal churches in other countries, the movement has always centered predominantly in the United States.

No one knows how many Pentecostals there are in the United States today, but the figure is well in excess of 2 million, and is growing very rapidly. Many religious authorities say that Pentecostal groups are expanding their membership at a faster rate than any other type of church.

The spread of the movement is illustrated in statistics of the General Council of the Assemblies of God, which is the largest and best-organized Pentecostal denomination. It was established in April, 1914, at a meeting of three hundred Pentecostal pastors and laymen at Hot Springs, Arkansas. By 1937, it had 3473 local congregations with a total of 175,362 members. Today there are more than 8000 Assembly of God churches in the United States, with a total membership of more than 500,000.

The Assemblies of God, like most Pentecostal bodies, place heavy emphasis on foreign missions, and now rank fifth among all U.S. denominations in the size of their missionary force abroad. They maintain nine colleges and Bible institutes in this country, and sixty-six Bible schools in other countries.

The next largest group of Pentecostals are the Churches of God. The *Yearbook of American Churches* lists nine different denominations with this title or some slight variation of it. Their total membership is about 400,000.

There are at least nine organized denominations with the word Pentecostal in their titles. They include the United Pentecostal Church, The Pentecostal Holiness Church, and The Pentecostal Church of God of America.

Thousands of local Pentecostal congregations are not affiliated with any denomination.

The Pentecostal movement is strongest in the South and West, but it has been growing fast lately in the Middle West.

THE HOLINESS CHURCHES

Historically related to the Pentecostal groups, and often confused with them in the public mind, are the so-called "holiness" churches, which are typified by the Church of the Nazarene.

The common bond of all the holiness denominations is a strong emphasis on John Wesley's doctrine of sanctification, which holds that the Holy Spirit achieves such a purifying of the hearts and motives of truly consecrated Christians that they are freed from their natural human proclivity toward sin and are rendered capable of perfect holiness, here and now, in this earthly life.

The more sedate of the holiness churches—such as the

Church of the Nazarene—do not practice tongue-speaking or any other outward manifestation of religious ecstasy. Their services are as decorous as even a Presbyterian could ask.

Nazarenes are almost as austere as old-time Quakers in their personal habits. The rules of the church forbid drinking, smoking, attendance at movies or plays, immodesty in dress or behavior, and any type of frivolity (even reading the newspapers) on Sunday.

But for all the strictness of their discipline, they do not seem to feel that holiness is burdensome. One is impressed in reading Nazarene literature by its constant emphasis on religion as a joyous experience.

Nazarenes attach great importance to personal evangelism, or "witnessing." They are also great givers. The church teaches the principle of tithing, and it is evident that a large proportion of the membership practices it: Nazarene contributions average more than twice the over-all average for Protestant denominations.

When it was founded on October 13, 1908, at Pilot Point, Texas, by the merger of two small regional Holiness Associations, the Church had only 10,414 members. Today it has nearly 300,000 members in North America, and an additional 45,000 in the forty foreign areas where Nazarene missionaries are at work.

JEHOVAH'S WITNESSES

America's fastest growing religious body is a Brooklyn-based sect whose adherents believe that Doomsday is hard at hand. Its official name is the Watchtower Bible and

Tract Society. The members are better known as Jehovah's Witnesses.

During the past twenty years—a period in which the membership of other churches approximately doubled—the number of Jehovah's Witnesses has increased by 700 per cent. Today there are about 900,000 full-fledged Witnesses, and perhaps an additional one million fringe members who read the Society's literature, attend its meetings, and generally sympathize with its doctrines. One third of them are in the United States. There also are fast-growing branches of the Society in West Germany, France, Latin America, and Africa.

Their phenomenal growth rate is the result of a zeal for evangelism that puts the established churches to shame. Every Witness is regarded as an ordained minister, and is sent out to ring doorbells, pass out literature on street corners, and preach the Society's message to as many people as possible. The average Witness, working an assigned territory, makes personal calls on at least ten homes each week.

Expectance of Armageddon

Behind this passion for convert-winning is the firm conviction of the Witnesses that the end of human history is imminent. They expect it to come at any hour, and almost certainly within the next ten years.

The end will come, they say, with a titanic Battle of Armageddon between the forces of God and the forces of Satan. The awesome pyrotechnics of this struggle "will make atomic explosions look like firecrackers." The only survivors will be Jehovah's Witnesses, who will thereafter live eternally and blissfully, not in heaven but right here on earth.

Because they regard all other religious bodies as instruments of Satan, Witnesses feel that they can express their love of neighbor only by relentless proselytizing—by bringing as many people as possible into their own fold before it is too late.

They also look upon all human governments as instruments of Satan, and therefore refuse to pledge allegiance to any flag or to serve in any nation's armed forces. This stand has brought them into constant conflict with the law, and exposed them to many mob attacks, tar-and-featherings and other savage persecutions, both in this country and elsewhere.

But the Witnesses are not adverse to using the judicial processes of government. Since 1938, they have carried fifty test cases before the United States Supreme Court and have won thirty-seven of them. Through this litigation they have won the right to preach on the streets, refuse jury duty, avoid salutes to the flag, and to carry on house-to-house solicitations.

Leading constitutional lawyers credit the cases brought by the Witnesses with achieving a major expansion of civil liberties for all Americans.

But this was a purely incidental by-product so far as the Witnesses are concerned. They care nothing for improving social conditions or righting injustice in human society, which they feel is corrupted beyond all hope of redemption and already doomed to fiery destruction.

Heaven for the Few Only

Witnesses or their literature have created the impression that they are an off-beat body of Protestants. But the Witnesses have a distinctive theology of their own, which can hardly be described as a version of Christianity.

In his excellent study of the Witnesses, *Armageddon Around the Corner* (The John Day Company, New York), Professor William J. Whalen, of Purdue University, says Witnesses may be described as "fundamentalist Unitarians."

"They regard the Bible as the infallible word of God, a word which must be taken literally and at face value," says Professor Whalen. "At the same time, they stoutly deny the divinity of Jesus Christ and the doctrine of the Trinity. An orthodox Christian theologian would recognize bits and pieces of a dozen ancient heresies in Witness theology."

Witnesses believe that the Almighty is wrathful at Christians because they call him God instead of using his proper name, Jehovah. They have their own translation of the Bible, in which the word Jehovah has been substituted for God more than six thousand times.

Although they look forward with joy to an imminent and fiery destruction of the present world, Witnesses do not believe in a hell. The wicked people who do not qualify for perpetual bliss after the Battle of Armageddon will not be condemned to eternal punishment. They will simply be extinguished.

Witness theology does provide for heaven, but only a

select "Little Flock" of 144,000 persons will go there. (This is based, like much Witness teaching, on an obscure passage in the Book of Revelation.) Others saved from the final debacle will remain on earth, enjoying a troublefree existence forever.

The official name of the Society is derived from the title of a magazine, *The Watchtower*, founded in 1879 by Charles Taze Russell, an Allegheny, Pennsylvania, haberdasher who was attracted to Adventist doctrines of biblical interpretation.

He acquired a body of followers, originally known as Russellites, and predicted that the world would come to an end in 1914. (Witness theologians have since reinterpreted his prophecy, and hold that 1914 marked the beginning of an "invisible struggle" in heaven that will culminate in the fiery Battle of Armageddon on earth, any day now.)

After Russell's death in 1916, the movement was headed by a Missouri lawyer, "Judge" Joseph F. Rutherford. He continued the emphasis on an imminent end of time, and was author of the famous Witness prophecy, "Millions now living will never die."

Rutherford died of cancer in 1942 and was succeeded by Nathan H. Knorr, of Bethlehem, Pennsylvania, who had been a full-time Witness since he graduated from high school in 1923.

Knorr is a quiet and retiring man compared to his colorful predecessors. He has been responsible for the present high degree of organizational efficiency in the Society, as well as for putting its prodigious output of literature (125 million books, tracts, and magazines a year) on a businesslike basis.

The Society's headquarters, called Bethel House, and its printing plant are located in Brooklyn. Full-time workers, of whom there are about five thousand in the movement, receive their room, board, and fourteen dollars a month spending money. Everyone, including President Knorr, lives on the same standard.

Other Witnesses earn their own living in everyday jobs and carry on their house-to-house evangelism during evenings and weekends. The movement in modern times has been notably devoid of scandals. Witnesses are excommunicated if they fail to maintain high standards of morality in their private lives.

CHAPTER IX

The Eastern Orthodox

A great many people, including journalists and public officials, labor under the delusion that America has only three major religious faiths—Protestant, Catholic, and Jewish.

This popular misapprehension is a source of considerable irritation to Americans who are members of the Eastern Orthodox Church. Eastern Orthodoxy is a major faith by any criterion, with a world-wide following of more than 150 million persons, including some 6 million in the United States.

Any attempt to lump Orthodox Christians with Protestants or Catholics is an egregious affront to the Orthodox. They not only regard their Church as an entirely separate branch of Christianity; they also insist that it is the one, true, original Christian church, "the depository and true preserver of early Christian faith."

They cite impressive historical evidence in support of this claim. The Christian church was born at the eastern end of the Mediterranean, and until it obtained a toe hold in the imperial capital of Rome, most of its apostolic activity was concentrated in that area. Jerusalem, Antioch, Corinth, and Alexandria were great centers of Christian worship long before the Roman Christians emerged from the catacombs. The Roman church grew rapidly in size and importance after it won imperial favor in the fourth century. Meanwhile, the Eastern churches increasingly looked for leadership to Constantinople, the transplanted capital of the Roman Empire. By A.D. 500 Rome had become the center of Christianity in the West, with Constantinople its center in the East.

The two branches of Christendom maintained the same creeds and sacraments, and their bishops came together occasionally for Ecumenical Councils, at which they sought (and usually achieved) agreement on doctrines affecting the whole Church. But over the centuries, they drifted progressively further apart. The Western churches used Latin in their liturgy, the Eastern churches used Greek. There were differences in ritual, with the Eastern churches preferring longer, more elaborate ceremonies than Western taste found congenial. But the really serious cause of friction was the growing persistence with which the Bishop of Rome claimed supreme authority over the universal Church.

The Great Schism

This claim was hotly disputed, not only by the Patriarch of Constantinople, but by most of the other bishops of the Eastern churches. By the time the last Ecumenical Council of the undivided Church was held, in A.D. 787, the issue was clearly drawn. The church of Rome asserted that Christ had entrusted the rule of the Church to St. Peter, and that Peter's authority descended by divine right to each man who succeeded him in the office of Bishop of Rome. The Eastern churches contended that Christ had never intended the Church to be under a centralized, monarchical government. On the contrary, they said, the early Christian churches founded in the Apostolic era all enjoyed a high degree of local autonomy. The Eastern churches were willing to extend a voluntary "primacy in honor" to the bishops of great metropolitan centers like Rome and Constantinople, but they declared that every bishop was equal in authority to every other bishop, and that only a synod, or council of all bishops, could presume to legislate for the entire Church.

In A.D. 1054 the estrangement was formalized by what historians have called "The Great Schism." The Roman Pope (Bishop of Rome) excommunicated the Patriarch of Constantinople, and the Patriarch excommunicated the Pope.

During the next century and a half, intermittent attempts were made to heal the breach. It is possible that some sort of accommodation might have been worked out. But in A.D. 1204 a contingent of Crusaders, en route from Italy to the Holy Land, stopped at Constantinople, sacked the city, pillaged its great Cathedral of St. Sophia, and installed a papal legatee on the Patriarch's throne.

From that day to this, millions of Orthodox Christians have felt toward the Pope of Rome very much as Americans of the Deep South feel toward General William Tecumseh Sherman.

In recent years, mighty efforts were made by the late

Pope John XXIII, and are still being made by Pope Paul VI, to overcome a millennium of distrust, and to pave the way for reunion of the Roman Catholic and Eastern Orthodox Churches. Pope John offered the Orthodox bishops seats of honor at the Second Vatican Council, and Pope Paul exchanged the "kiss of peace" with the Patriarch of Constantinople in a dramatic personal meeting at Jerusalem. Some Orthodox leaders have responded warmly to these overtures, but others remain coolly suspicious. Even the most ecumenical-minded Orthodox say that reunion is out of the question until the Pope is prepared to accept the status of "first among equals." And there is no prospect of the Pope's accepting that status any time soon—to put it mildly.

Orthodox and Catholic Similarities

Although they are poles apart on the question of papal authority, the Eastern Orthodox Church and the Roman Catholic Church are very close together on other doctrinal matters. The Orthodox Eucharist, known as the Divine Liturgy, is fundamentally similar to the Catholic Mass. The most conspicuous differences are that the Byzantine rites are much longer (sometimes running to three hours) and more colorful; the Orthodox use bread made with yeast for Communion, whereas Roman Catholics use a wafer made of unleavened flour and water; and the Orthodox laity receive Communion in both kinds—that is, they partake of the consecrated wine as well as the bread, while Catholics receive only the latter (except in very special circumstances). The Orthodox Church has for many centuries permitted use of vernacular languages in congregational worship—a reform that the Second Vatican Council decreed for Roman Catholic Churches in 1963.

Like Catholics, the Orthodox observe seven sacraments: baptism, confirmation, penance, the Eucharist, holy orders, matrimony, and extreme unction. Baptism is administered by triple immersion, and is followed immediately by the rite of confirmation, which is called Holy Chrismation.

The Orthodox Church ordains married men to the priesthood, but once ordained a priest may not marry. Only celibates are eligible for consecration as bishops. The Roman Catholic Church recognizes the validity of Eastern Orthodox priestly orders, and a Catholic who is near death and unable to find a Catholic priest may make his confession to and receive extreme unction from an Orthodox priest. Orthodox priests are addressed as "Father."

For Orthodox, as for Catholics, every Friday is a day of abstinence from meat, in commemoration of Christ's sacrifice on Calvary. The Orthodox Church observes substantially the same holy days as the Catholic Church, but because of an ancient and complicated difference in the method of calculating the date of Easter, the Orthodox celebration of that festival, and of all the other liturgical holidays that are tied to it, often differs by as much as two or three weeks from the calendar of Western churches.

Orthodox worship has a strong mystical bent. One of its distinctive aspects is the widespread use in churches and homes of sacred images of Christ and the saints. These images—they may be paintings or mosaics—are called icons. Their purpose is to emphasize the living reality of the persons they depict. Praying before an icon, an Orthodox Christian is reminded that Jesus is not an empty name, nor an abstract concept, but one who was incarnate (embodied in human flesh and blood), and who still lives and reigns as Lord among his people. "There is in the Orthodox Church a strong feeling of the reality of the supernatural," says one of its scholars. "There is no death, but life, whether upon the earth or beyond it."

Orthodox Christians venerate all saints, and they rival Catholics in their devotion to the Virgin Mary. They regard Mary as the holiest of human beings, but do not subscribe to the Catholic dogma of the Immaculate Conception, which holds that Mary was preserved from the taint of original sin from the moment she was conceived in her mother's womb. The Orthodox also reject the Catholic belief in purgatory, for which they find no warrant either in Scripture or in sacred tradition as it was defined by the Ecumenical Councils of the undivided Church.

It is a matter of fundamental importance to Orthodoxy neither to add to nor subtract from the "original Christianity" that the Apostles taught, and which the early Church sought to express both in its Scriptures and its creeds, sacraments, and liturgies. Indeed, that is what the term Orthodox means; it is compounded of two Greek words meaning "right faith."

"The Orthodox Church today teaches exactly the same message which was taught by the undivided Church for a thousand years," says the Reverend Demetrious J. Constantelos, a prominent American Orthodox scholar. "Nothing has been added, and nothing has been deleted following the Great Schism. In the twentieth century, the Orthodox Church remains the original depository and true preserver of early Christian faith, culture and life, which were universally accepted and attested to in the early centuries of our era."

Orthodox theologians feel that the Roman Catholic Church has distorted the original Christian faith by adding to it, and that Protestant denominations have gone astray by deleting essential doctrines.

Although their adamant claim to be the one true Church makes the Orthodox somewhat difficult to get along with in ecumenical gatherings, they have shown a willingness in recent years to cooperate with major Protestant bodies in practical matters, and at least to discuss doctrinal questions with them. The major Orthodox bodies are members of the National Council of Churches in the United States, and of the World Council of Churches.

Although Orthodox Christians are bound together by a common spiritual heritage, they have no central organizational structure. The Patriarch of Constantinople enjoys a "primacy of honor," but he has no real authority outside of his own severely shrunken patriarchate in the city that is now known as Istanbul. Applying to modern geography the principle of autonomy, which it has always upheld, the Orthodox Communion is composed today of a dozen self-governing ("autocephalous") national churches. The largest of these is found in Russia, where Orthodoxy was the state religion under the czars, and where it still claims some 50 million adherents after two generations of persecution by the Communist regime.

There also are large Orthodox churches in several other Iron Curtain countries, including Romania, Yugoslavia,

Bulgaria, Poland, Czechoslovakia, and Albania. All labor under varying degrees of persecution.

Greece is now the only country in which the Orthodox Church enjoys the status of official state religion. The Greek Orthodox Church has about 9 million members.

The Orthodox in America

The Orthodox faith came to America with immigrants from many countries of Eastern Europe and the Mediterranean. The first Orthodox Church on what is now American soil was built by Russian monks at Kodiak, Alaska, in 1792. Before Alaska passed into United States hands, the Russian monks won many converts among the Eskimos, and built a cathedral that is still in use in Sitka.

Since each group of immigrants brought with them their particular national expression of Orthodoxy, America by the start of the twentieth century had a bewildering variety of Orthodox churches—Russian, Greek, Serbian, Syrian, Polish, Romanian, and so on. At first they had relatively little to do with one another. In recent years, however, they have begun to draw together, and some leaders believe that the time is rapidly approaching when they will merge into a single American Orthodox Church.

CHAPTER X

Islam and the Moslems

The youngest of the world's major religions, and the only one that seriously rivals Christianity in international missionary outreach, is the faith which the prophet Mohammed introduced among the Arabs in the seventh century.

Its correct name is *Islam*, an Arabic word meaning "submission to the will of God." Its adherents are called *Moslems* (in Arabic, *Muslim*), which means "those who submit to the will of God."

Moslems are mortally insulted when people refer to them as "Mohammedans." They feel that this term implies that they worship Mohammed. And nothing could be further from the truth. Islam is a fiercely monotheistic religion, and while it reveres Mohammed as the last and greatest of the prophets, it has been unswervingly faithful to the creed that is the heart of Mohammed's teaching: "There is no God but Allah."

The Prophet of Allah

Mohammed was born about A.D. 570 in the city of Mecca, in what is now the country of Saudi Arabia. A camel driver by profession, he made a number of caravan trips to

Jerusalem, where he became familiar with Judaism and Christianity.

Mohammed was deeply moved by the concept of a benevolent, omnipotent God which he encountered in Jewish and Christian scriptures. The Arab tribes of his day were pagan idol-worshipers. They thought that the world was infested with many gods, who were apt to turn hostile unless buttered up by animal sacrifices and other ritual acts. The one moderately benign deity in the Arab pantheon was known as Allah, and until Mohammed came along, no one paid very much mind to him.

To challenge the paganism of his people was no easy thing for Mohammed. His city of Mecca was a center of pilgrimage for Bedouin tribes, and the local population made a nice living off the tourists who came to worship at the various idol shrines.

Faced with conflict between a dawning conviction and the whole culture in which he lived, Mohammed did what Jesus had done seven centuries earlier. He withdrew into the wilderness to fast, pray, and ponder. Mohammed's particular retreat was a cave near Mecca. Over a period of at least ten years, and perhaps longer, he visited the cave at frequent intervals. There, he said, he was visited by the Angel Gabriel, who opened his eyes to the errors of Judaism and Christianity, and told him that he had been chosen for the task of correcting and completing the divine revelation which was begun in the older faiths.

Mohammed emerged from this period of spiritual gestation with a message that burst upon the Arab world like a bombshell. Allah, he said, is the only God there is. He created the universe and has absolute, unchallenged, unshared dominion over it. And He is no distant, malevolent Being who scorns man and his problems. He is "gracious, compassionate, near at hand, merciful, forgiving, the shelterer of the orphan, the guide of the erring, the friend of the bereaved, the consoler of the afflicted." His love for man "is more tender than that of the mother bird for her young."

Mohammed readily acknowledged that Jews and Christians had been worshiping Allah, under a different name, for many centuries. He accepted in full the Old Testament story of Abraham, and claimed that Arabs, as well as Jews, were descended from the Patriarch. (The Arab ancestor was said to be Ishmael, the son of Hagar, whom Abraham was forced to banish after his long-barren first wife, Sarah, finally bore him a son named Isaac.) Mohammed also accorded the status of true prophets to other leading biblical figures, including Moses and Jesus. Indeed, Mohammed showed a particular reverence for Jesus, accepting much of what the New Testament says about him, including the statement that he was born of a virgin.

But Mohammed emphatically rejected the one really basic thing that Christians believe about Jesus: that he was the incarnate Son of God. Mohammed also dismissed entirely the New Testament accounts of Jesus' crucifixion and resurrection. Although he regarded Jesus simply as a human prophet, Mohammed felt that God would never have allowed such a prophet to be put to death cruelly on a cross. Therefore Islam holds that Jesus was taken up into heaven without undergoing death.

The Koran

The revelations that Mohammed brought forth from the cave near Mecca were written down by scribes in a book called the Koran (from an Arabic word for "reading matter"). Orthodox Moslems look upon the Koran as fundamentalist Christians look upon the Bible—as the verbally inspired, completely infallible Word of God. The Koran is divided into 114 chapters, or *surahs*, which are arranged in descending order of length, with the longest first and the shortest last. The over-all wordage is slightly less than that of the New Testament. Moslems contend that the Koran can be properly read only in its original language—Arabic —and whereas Christians have translated their Scriptures into more than one thousand languages, Moslems have concentrated on teaching their converts to read Arabic.

All but one of the *surahs* open with the same words: "In the name of Allah, the Beneficent, the Merciful!" This phrase is the keynote of the Koran, which is primarily concerned with assuring men of the oneness, the nearness and the goodness of God.

The theology of Islam, as laid down in the Koran, is simple and straightforward: Those who do right in this life will go to heaven; those who do wrong will go to hell. The Koran contains vivid descriptions of both destinations. Heaven is depicted as a place where there are pleasant gardens, cool fountains, lavish mansions, and all sorts of entertainments, including plenty of lovely dark-eyed girls. Hell is a fiery furnace, swept by "pestilential winds," and bubbling with molten liquids.

"The Five Pillars of Islam"

The Koran also tells a Moslem precisely what he must do to qualify for admission to heaven. He must perform five religious duties, which Mohammed called "The Five Pillars of Islam."

The first is to say aloud, with full understanding and complete conviction, the Islamic creed: *"La ilah illa Allah, Mohammed rasulu Allah"* ("There is no God but Allah, and Mohammed is His prophet"). Technically, it is sufficient to say the creed once in a lifetime (as on a deathbed), but devout Moslems actually repeat it many times every day.

The second duty is to face Mecca and pray, five times daily—at sunrise, at noon, in the early afternoon, at sunset, and at the fall of darkness. During these prayers, a Moslem assumes certain prescribed positions of kneeling and bowing. He is expected to pray at the proper hours regardless of where he may be—even if he is crossing the Atlantic in a jet airliner. On Friday—the Islamic Sabbath—Moslems go to a mosque for corporate worship.

The third Pillar of Islam is charity. Mohammed laid great stress on compassion toward the poor, and the Koran stipulates that each Moslem must set aside annually 2½ per cent of his total wealth (not 2½ per cent of his annual income, but of his entire capital) to be distributed among the poor.

The fourth duty is to fast during the holy month of Ramadan, the ninth month of the Moslem year. The fast is extremely rigorous. From earliest sunrise—as soon as it is light enough "for a white thread to be distinguished from a dark thread"—until sunset, a keeper of the fast may not eat or drink (not even a sip of water), or engage in sexual relations. After the sunset, the rules are relaxed—but even then, good Moslems are expected to practice "moderation." When the Fast of Ramadan falls during the winter, when days are short, it is much less difficult for Moslems than when it falls during the long days of summer. Many Moslems get through the observance by sleeping away most of the daylight hours. As a result, normal business, government, and educational activities tend to come to a halt during the month of Ramadan.

Finally, every Moslem who is physically and financially able to do so is required to make a pilgrimage to Mecca at least once in his lifetime.

The Pilgrimage to Mecca

Mecca is sacred to Islam not only as the birthplace of the Prophet, but also because it contains the one ancient shrine which Mohammed did not abolish when he declared war against idolatry. It is called the Holy Kaaba. It is a massive, cubelike edifice of stone, veiled in blue-black cloth, and situated in the center of a great courtyard. Moslems believe that it marks the site of the first house of worship on earth—the temple at which Adam prayed after he was expelled from the Garden of Eden. According to Islamic legend, the Kaaba was destroyed by the great flood in the time of Noah, and was later rebuilt on the same spot by Abraham. Its holiest object is a black stone, resembling a large meteorite, which is set in the southeast corner of the Kaaba. In the old pagan days, Arabs worshiped this stone as a god. Mohammed allowed them to continue venerating it, but explained that it was worthy of respect because it was brought by the Angel Gabriel to assist Abraham in the rebuilding of the Kaaba.

Each year in the season of the great pilgrimage, more than 500,000 Moslems from all parts of the world converge on Mecca to trot seven times around the Kaaba and kiss the black stone. In addition to the prescribed seven circuits of the Kaaba, a pilgrim's itinerary includes visits to other holy places, including the Plain of Arafat twenty-five miles from Mecca, where, according to legend, Adam and Eve were reunited after their expulsion from the Garden of Eden, and where Mohammed preached his final sermon before his death in A.D. 632.

Moslems also cherish the city of Medina, 220 miles north of Mecca, which gave refuge to Mohammed when, at the start of his ministry, he was driven out of Mecca by merchants who resented his assault on the city's chief industry, idol worship. Mohammed's Hegira, or flight from Mecca, occurred in A.D. 622. It is regarded as the turning point in the history of Islam, and marks the beginning of year 1 on the Moslem calendar.

The Moral Rules

In addition to the Five Pillars of Islam, Mohammed laid down a number of other moral rules for his followers. He forbade drinking, gambling, the eating of pork, and the acceptance of interest on loans. These rules are still obeyed by some strict Moslems, but they have been considerably relaxed in more liberal Moslem circles, where they are regarded as time-conditioned exhortations that were necessary in Mohammed's day, but that are not of the same unchanging and eternal nature as the Five Pillars.

Christians are often scandalized by Mohammed's marriage rules. The Prophet said that a man might take up to four wives, provided he could afford to support them. He said that a husband could divorce a wife by saying to her on three separate occasions, "I divorce thee," and by giving her a suitable financial settlement.

These rules actually represented a tremendous advance in the status of women in the Arab culture of Mohammed's day. Previously, women had been little more than chattel, and no one took marriage seriously enough to bother counting his wives or going through any formality whatever when he wished to chase one off. Females were held in such low esteem that girl babies often were buried alive.

Mohammed strictly forbade the murder of girl babies, and went so far as to require that daughters be permitted to share with sons in the division of an inheritance—a revolutionary step in the Arabic world. While he permitted polygamy, he made adultery punishable by death, and provided a whole range of cultural safeguards (including purdah, or veiling) to protect women from lascivious exploitation.

Islam's toleration of polygamy is one of the three great advantages it holds over Christianity in their current competition for converts in Black Africa. Another advantage is that Islam's record in race relations—and particularly in acceptance of dark-skinned peoples into full fellowship—is as good as Christianity's is bad. Both Jesus and Mohammed taught that all men are brothers, but Mohammed's followers have always taken the doctrine seriously, whereas those who proclaim the name of Jesus have only recently and timidly begun to act as if they really believed that whites and blacks are brothers.

Islam's third advantage is that every Moslem—be he trader, diplomat, or tourist—considers himself a missionary, responsible for spreading the true faith wherever he goes. Several American Protestant bodies have tried in recent years to implant the same idea in the minds of laymen going abroad on government or private business, but without conspicuous success.

The Expansion of Islam

Considering all these advantages, it is no surprise to learn that Islam is winning ten times as many converts as Christianity in the newly emergent nations south of the Sahara. While accurate statistics are lacking, some studies indicate that a third of Africa's 200 million people are now Moslems.

Islam has no hierarchic priesthood. Mosque services are conducted by an *imam*, a title which simply means "leader." Some Islamic sects have full-time, paid imams, comparable to Protestant pastors. But the imam is often a local business or professional man who is well-versed in the Koran.

Koranic scholars are held in great reverence. Although there is no central authority in Islam to decide questions of doctrine, many Moslems accord to Al Azhar University in Cairo a unique eminence in the preservation and interpretation of Islamic orthodoxy.

During Mohammed's lifetime, Islam was an Arab religion, virtually unknown outside of the Middle Eastern land in which it was born. But within a year after Mohammed's death, it had burst out of the Arabian Peninsula and was sweeping north, east, and west. The military victories of Arab armies (who threatened to conquer all of Western Europe until Charles Martel turned back their advance at the historic Battle of Tours in A.D. 732) unquestionably helped pave the way for the spread of the Islamic faith—just as European colonial conquests opened large areas of the world to Christian missionaries. But Moslems bitterly resent the charge, casually made in many Western history books, that Islam won converts at sword's point. They point out that the Koran firmly admonishes: "Let there be no compulsion in religion," and they assert that this precept was observed in the toleration extended to Jews and Christians under Arab rule. In any case, they say, Christians have a lot of nerve talking about anyone else's using violence as a weapon of evangelism. Remember the Crusades?

Within a century after Mohammed's death, the boundaries of Islam stretched from Spain and Morocco in the West, to India and China in the East.

Today there are upwards of 400 million Moslems in the world. Only about 10 per cent of them live in the Arab countries of the Middle East. There are huge Moslem populations in Pakistan, Indonesia, Iran, and Turkey, and sizable numbers in Nigeria, the Sudan, Russia, India, Kenya, Uganda, and in the new nations of West Africa.

According to the Islamic Center in Washington, D.C. (which has its headquarters in a lovely mosque on Massachusetts Avenue that has become one of the capital's chief tourist attractions), there are about 100,000 true Moslems in the United States. Most of them are immigrants from Islamic countries, but there also are about 3000 American Negroes who have become converts to Islam.

These bona fide Negro Moslems are not to be confused with members of the so-called Black Muslim sect headed by a man who calls himself Elijah Muhammed. The Black Muslims adopt Moslem names, wear fezzes, and use a certain amount of Islamic ritual and language, but they are not true Moslems. For one thing, their chief doctrine—implacable hatred of white men—is contrary to the historic Islamic teaching that all men are brothers, regardless of race. Also, Elijah Muhammed has committed what any orthodox Moslem regards as the worst kind of heresy by billing himself as a prophet. It is a cardinal dogma of Islam that Mohammed was the last prophet, and that there will be no more after him.

CHAPTER XI

The Oriental Religions

We have a tendency in the West to swing violently from one extreme to the other in our appraisal of anything Oriental. For example, before the Korean War most of us held a very low opinion of Red China's military power. Today, many regard it as the greatest menace confronting the free world.

A similar flip-flop has occurred in our attitude toward Oriental religions. Not too many years back, we were looking down on them as pagan idolatries. Now we're inclined to speak of them with awesome respect. In some intellectual and pseudo-intellectual circles, you are not *au courant* unless you can speak knowingly about the Bhagavad-Gita, or recite a Zen *Koan*.

The two attitudes have one thing in common: both are based on ignorance. We used to sneer at what were really caricatures of the Oriental religions. Now we are adulating what are really highly idealized portraits of them.

In this chapter we'll try to take an honest, unbiased look at the ancient faith of *Hinduism*, and its thriving offshoot, *Buddhism*. We'll look at them respectfully, recognizing the important role they have played in human history and acknowledging gratefully the profound truths and insights they offer. But we shall hopefully avoid the current vogue of romanticizing them to the point where their own adherents would scarcely know them.

HINDUISM

Hinduism is the religion of India. It seems to have originated about four thousand years ago in the valley of the Indus River (from which it got its name). It has never done well on foreign soil. Today there are some 300 million Hindus in India, but only about 15 million outside it—and most of the latter are in neighboring lands, such as Pakistan, Ceylon, and Burma, which have been heavily influenced by Indian culture.

There is no central figure in Hinduism who occupies a place comparable to that of Jesus Christ in Christianity or Gautama Buddha in Buddhism. Nor does Hinduism claim to have received any special revelation from God. The scriptures of Hinduism are a vast, unorganized collection of writings that represent the speculations of thousands of different sages at many different periods of history. The oldest of these writings, the Vedas (a Sanskrit word meaning divine knowledge), date from about 1000 B.C., and perhaps earlier. The Upanishads, which are philosophical treatises, and the two great epic poems, Mahabharata and Ramayana, came along some centuries later. The Mahabharata is best known for one of its subdivisions, the Bhagavad-Gita (Song of the Blessed One), which tells how the god Vishnu appeared on a battlefield to give philosophical instruction to a warrior named Arjuna, who was wondering why he should go forth to kill or be killed. Those who have gotten the impression from the teaching of Mahatma Gandhi that nonviolence is a cardinal principle of Hinduism will find this poem quite startling, since the burden of Vishnu's advice is to get in there and fight.

Beware of people who try to prove any statement about Hinduism by quoting from these scriptures. Tolerance of many different points of view is one of the most characteristic traits of Hinduism, and when sages disagreed, as they often did, the Hindus simply included both opinions in the sacred writings. This makes generalizations about them more than usually precarious.

Another reason why it is rash to reach sweeping conclusions about Hinduism after reading a few excerpts from the Vedas and a blank-verse English translation of the Bhagavad-Gita, is that a great gulf exists between the philosophical Hinduism that we encounter in these scriptures, and the popular Hinduism that is actually practiced in the villages of India. The latter always has been, and still is, a polytheistic religion that rises little, if at all, above the level of primitive idol-worship.

With these caveats, let us proceed gingerly to a description of the Hindu world-view as it has been expounded by most of the sages.

Its basic tenet is the oneness of all things. There is only one ultimate reality—*Brahman*. Brahman is pure, unchanging, eternal, impersonal spirit. From Brahman emanates *maya*—a term which encompasses the whole created universe, and which also has connotations of illusion and deception. Maya has only that kind of reality which objects in a dream have for the person who is dreaming. The visible world is actually insubstantial and transitory, and man's separate existence is an illusion. The only worthwhile objective that a man can pursue is to escape from the illusion of existence and be swallowed up in the Oneness of Brahman, as a river returns to the sea.

The Concept of Reincarnation

But escape is not easy. It cannot be achieved merely by committing suicide. For the world of maya is governed by an iron law of retribution, known as *karma*. This law decrees that every man must "eat the fruit of his deeds," no matter how many lifetimes it may require. The doctrine of karma is closely related to the Hindu concept of reincarnation. Individual bits of life begin very low in the scale, as insects. They progress upward, more or less automatically, through various incarnations in animal form, until they attain the threshold of self-awareness which we call humanity. From this point onward, a person's future life depends irrevocably on how he behaves in his present life. If he is guilty of serious misdeeds, or neglects his spiritual progress, he will be reborn in a lower station. He may even backslide all the way to animalhood. On the other hand, if he lives a correct life and works steadily at the renunciation of worldly desires, he will be reincarnated in a higher status. And ultimately, he can break away entirely from the "wheel of existence" and lose his individual identity in reunion with the All-One.

This doctrine provides Hinduism with a ready explanation for all inequality and human suffering. And it enables devout upper-class Hindus to shrug off the misery of the Indian masses. Of all the differences between Christianity and Hinduism, this is perhaps the most profound. Whereas Christ reached out in compassion to the poor and hungry, and proclaimed them especially blessed in the eyes of God, Hinduism teaches that they are merely getting their just desserts.

The unquestioning acceptance of this viewpoint by nearly all Indians is one of the greatest obstacles that Christian missionaries have encountered. Steeped in a culture which takes karma for granted, Indians are scandalized, to a degree no Westerner can begin to appreciate, when Christians candidly admit that Christ died in agony on a cross. But a more recent historical event has caused some second thoughts about karma. Mahatma Gandhi was universally revered as a holy man and even the most devout Hindu found it hard to regard his brutal slaying by an assassin as the just fruit of past misdeeds.

The Caste System

The social expression of the doctrine of karma is India's caste system, which has proved stubbornly resistant to change. At the top of the heap are members of the highest or priestly caste, the Brahmans, who are considered to be well on their way toward the goal of final escape from life. There are three other major castes—warriors, artisans, and laborers—and some three thousand subcastes. Finally, there are about 50 million Indians, the so-called "untouchables," who are literally the "out-castes" of Indian society, not being members of any of the recognized stratifications.

The caste into which a Hindu is born determines to a large degree what kind of work he will do, how much education he will get, what kind of home he will live in, and how far he can expect to go in life. It even affects his love life, since marriage across caste lines is prohibited by a taboo vastly stronger than United States laws against interracial marriages.

Hindu beliefs about karma and reincarnation also are reflected—more attractively to Western observers—in the great consideration that Indians show to animals. Since every man was once an animal, and every animal will someday be a man, the Hindu finds it inexcusable that a man should ever willfully mistreat an animal. Cows rank highest in Hindu esteem, and one of the Vedas warns that anyone who kills a cow will be punished for as many years as there are hairs on the cow's body.

Two other major differences between Hinduism and Christianity deserve notice.

One of them might be summarized by saying that Christianity affirms life, whereas Hinduism denies it. The great promise of Christianity is "life eternal." The great goal of Hinduism is to escape from the "wheel of existence." Christianity holds out the hope of survival of the individual personality after death. Hinduism looks forward to the final loss of the "illusion" of personal identity.

These radically different views of man's destiny are closely related to an equally basic disagreement about the nature of ultimate reality. Christians look upon personality —that is, the state of self-conscious, purposeful being—as the highest thing they have encountered in the universe. It is therefore natural for them to think of God as having the attributes of personhood, and to speak of him in personal pronouns. But it is axiomatic among Hindus that the impersonal is higher than the personal. Brahman, to a Hindu sage, is always "It" or "That"—never "He." This does *not* mean that Hinduism has no personal gods. It has literally millions of them. All are regarded as emanating from Brahman. Although some of them have exceedingly long life spans—running into billions of years —they are not considered to be eternal, self-sufficient spirits. Some are thought to be benignly disposed toward human creatures; others are felt to be malevolent. The latter are of particular concern to village Hinduism.

At the head of the Hindu pantheon are Brahma, the Creator; Vishnu, the Preserver; and Shiva, the Destroyer. Popular piety tends to ignore Brahma, and most Hindus belong either to the sect of Vishnu or to that of Shiva. There also is a substantial cult for Shiva's wife, Shakti, who is the goddess in charge of epidemics, earthquakes, and floods.

Hindu religious practice, like Hindu doctrine, runs the gamut from the very primitive to the highly sophisticated. The primitive versions, which predominate in the villages, include rituals of propitiation and sacrifice before figures of the gods and goddesses. At the sophisticated end of the scale we find the high developed system of mysticism and ascetic discipline known as *yoga*.

There are several different varieties of yoga.* In general, the objective is to bring the mind and body under such

* You'll find a detailed description of the various types of yoga in Huston Smith's admirable book *The Religions of Man* (Harper & Row Publishers, New York).

a high degree of control that the practitioner (called a *yogi*) can escape from the distractions of sense perception and achieve a state of complete union with the all-pervading Reality, Brahman. Yogis who have undergone long years of intensive self-discipline can do things that seem incredible to the rest of us—such as lying on beds of nails, walking on hot coals, and holding their breath for an hour.

Except as a subject for dilettante discussion, Hinduism has never achieved more than a toe hold in the United States. But there are two organized groups dedicated to the furtherance of Hindu religious beliefs. One is The Theosophical Society of America. Founded in 1891, it maintains a national headquarters in Wheaton, Illinois, and has several thousand members. The other is The Vedanta Society, which was organized in 1893 by a Hindu missionary to America, Swami Abhedananda. It has a headquarters in New York and branches in ten other cities, with a total membership of perhaps two thousand.

BUDDHISM

Buddhism is sometimes called "Hindu Protestantism." It originated in India 2500 years ago as a protest or reform movement within Hinduism.

Its founder was an enormously wealthy Indian prince, Siddhartha Gautama, who was born about 560 B.C. in a northern province about one hundred miles from Benares. Legend says that Gautama had three palaces and forty thousand dancing girls to keep him amused. But he learned early in life that luxury did not lead to happiness. When he was about twenty-nine years old, he abandoned his sumptuous life as a prince and went into the forest, dressed in rags, to seek enlightenment in the solitary life of a Hindu ascetic.

No one ever practiced mortification of the flesh with greater dedication than Gautama. He fasted (eating one bean a day) until his spine could be seen through his shrunken stomach. But he found no answers to his questions about life, and concluded that extreme asceticism was no better than luxury as a pathway to happiness.

After six years of futile searching, Gautama seated himself one evening beneath the shade of a fig tree near the village of Gaya in northeast India. He vowed that he would sit right there until he saw the light.

According to Buddhist scriptures, he remained in meditation for forty-nine days. He emerged from this experience as the Buddha, or the "Enlightened One." For the next forty-five years, he walked from one Indian village to another, sharing his new insights with all who would listen, and founding an order of monks to practice his precepts and pass on his message. He died at the age of eighty after eating some poisoned mushrooms that had gotten into a dish by accident.

The earliest Buddhist scriptures record Buddha's teachings, usually in the form of dialogues between the Master and his disciples. In these records, we encounter a gracious and compassionate man of great personal charm. Buddha was always serene, courteous, and genuinely concerned for others. His wisdom was liberally seasoned with wit. It is small wonder that he acquired a large following during his lifetime, or that he continues to exert a strong attraction on thoughtful people from the West as well as the East.

Buddha did not invent a brand-new religion, any more than did Martin Luther. Just as Protestantism maintained many of the central concepts of Catholic Christianity, Buddhism retained the fundamental Hindu doctrines of karma and reincarnation. What Buddha tried to do (and the parallel with Luther is again striking) was to purge Hinduism of the polytheistic idol-worship, the superstitious rituals, and the oppressive caste system that had overlaid and obscured the original insights of the ancient Hindu sages.

The "Four Noble Truths"

At the heart of Buddha's teaching were the "Four Noble Truths," which he expounded in his first sermon and kept reiterating throughout his life. He asserted that:

(1) Human existence is universally characterized by suffering.

(2) The basic cause of suffering is *tanha* (a word that is often translated as "desire," but which actually connotes selfish craving, the tendency in every person to seek his own private happiness).

(3) Release from suffering can be achieved by the elimination of selfish craving.

(4) Craving cannot be eliminated by rigorous asceticism (as the Hindu yogis thought). The secret lies in following a middle way between asceticism and self-indulgence. This middle way Buddha called the "Eightfold Path."

The Eightfold Path consists of right knowledge, right aspiration, right speech, right behavior, right occupation, right effort, right thinking, and right absorption.

Under each of these eight broad headings, Buddha laid down rigorous rules of personal conduct for his disciples to follow. They were forbidden to lie, steal, or harm any living creature, including animals and insects. (Buddhist monks to this day strain their drinking water, lest they inadvertently swallow and destroy some minute creature.) They were allowed to eat only what they could beg, and then just enough to keep the body alive and functioning. Alcoholic beverages and sex relations were strictly forbidden. Most of their time was to be spent in philosophical discourse on the Four Noble Truths, and in private meditation.

Buddha said that this monastic way of life, if earnestly practiced, would lead eventually to *Nirvana*. Exactly what he meant by this much-abused term is hard to determine from his authenticated sayings. At times he seems to think of *Nirvana* as a final extinction of human individuality, comparable to the blowing out of a flame. Other Buddhist scriptures depict Nirvana as a blissful state, which would seem to imply the survival of some self-conscious identity to be aware of bliss.

It is even harder to determine what Buddha believed about God. Reacting against the lush growth of metaphysical speculation in the Hinduism of his day, Buddha was extremely reluctant to talk about such things as the origins of the universe, or the nature of ultimate reality. In one of his sermons, he does refer to "an Unborn One, not become, not made, uncompounded." This passage is often quoted to show that Buddha did believe in God. But if he did, he certainly had no place in his philosophy for a God who enters into personal relationships with human creatures and who is concerned with their fate. The Eight-fold Path is a plan for self-salvation, in which man is entirely on his own.

Two Distinct Kinds of Buddhism

After Buddha's death, his followers split into two schools, which have drifted so far apart over the centuries as to become virtually two different religions. They are known, respectively, as *Hinayana* ("Little Raft") and *Mahayana* ("Big Raft") *Buddhism*. Hinayana Buddhism is found to-day primarily in Ceylon, Burma, Viet-Nam, Thailand, Laos, Cambodia, and other parts of Southeast Asia. Maha-yana Buddhism prevails in Japan, Korea, China, Mongolia, and Tibet.

Of the two versions, Hinayana is unquestionably much closer to the Buddha's original teachings. It is an austere religion, for all practical purposes atheistic, and its re-quirements for renunciation of the world are so severe that it can be fully practiced only in a monastic environment. In Hinayana countries, men who take their Buddhism seriously shave their heads, put on saffron robes, divest themselves of all property except a staff and a begging bowl, and go forth to live as monks. The ideal of Hinayana is the solitary holy man who has attained enlightenment for himself. That's why it is called the "little raft" religion: its emphasis is on each man getting himself across the river of life to the safe harbor of Nirvana.

Mahayana Buddhists pay less attention to the teachings and more to the living example of Buddha. They point out that he did not cross over into Nirvana after he achieved enlightenment for himself, but returned to share his discovery with other men, so that they might join him on a "big raft."

Whereas Hinayana exalts wisdom and self-control, the great virtues for Mahayana are compassion and self-giving.

The most striking difference between the two versions of Buddha, however, is in their attitude toward Buddha himself. Hinayana is faithful to Buddha's own description of himself as an ordinary mortal who achieved enlightenment. Mahayana looks upon Buddha as a god who lived for a time on earth and who now looks down in pity upon human beings from a heavenly paradise. The influence of Christianity upon Mahayana Buddhism is clearly apparent. Not only have Mahayana Buddhists taken over such Christian concepts as faith, forgiveness, grace, and salvation (always substituting Buddha for Christ), but they have even adopted such terms as saint, bishop, reverend, and catechism. Indeed, one Christian missionary solemnly reports having heard a class of Buddhist children singing, "Buddha loves me, this I know. . . ."

The Real Zen

Zen Buddhism, which has enjoyed a vogue in certain Western circles in recent years, is a special case. It developed in China in the sixth century A.D., and by the twelfth century had reached Japan, where it has some 9 billion adherents today. The heart of Zen is the conviction that real truth can never be expressed or understood in verbal formulas, but can only be directly experienced through a flash of intuition called *satori*. To drive home the lesson that rationality and language are barriers rather than pathways to enlightenment, Zen masters require their students to spend endless hours working on *koans*, which are nonsense problems to which there are no rational solutions. True Zen is an austere, monastic religion, which has much in common with some varieties of Christian mysticism. It can be practiced in earnest only by men who are prepared to renounce the world and spend many years in intense meditation. The beatnik poets who try to mix a little Zen jargon with their beer, or the slightly cleaner "intellectuals" who use drugs like mescalin to achieve a cheap synthetic imitation of a Zen trance are insulting rather than embracing this old and respectable branch of Buddhism.

Buddhism has no hierarchy, no central organization, and no statistical offices. Guesses as to the number of Buddhists in the world today range from 150 million to 500 million. Although Buddhism, like Christianity, has been a missionary religion since its inception, it has remained concentrated in Asia. Ironically, it has very few adherents today in the land of its birth, India. Hinduism absorbed some of Buddha's teachings, and added Buddha himself to the extensive list of Hindu gods. Within a few centuries, the parent-religion had simply swallowed up its "Protestant offshoot" in India, and Buddhism developed as a separate faith only in other countries.

Like Islam and Hinduism, Buddhism has experienced a considerable renascence in recent years as a result of the wave of nationalism sweeping the nonwhite nations. In some Asian countries, adherence to the "native" religion, as opposed to the "white man's export," Christianity, is regarded as a mark of patriotism and anticolonial fervor.

Buddhism has perhaps three hundred thousand adherents in the United States. Most of them are Americans of Japanese descent, and more than half of them live in Hawaii, where Buddhists constitute the largest single religious group. According to the American Buddhist Association, which has its headquarters in Chicago, there also are more than fifty organized Buddhist congregations in mainland United States cities. The vast majority of America's Buddhists belong to the Mahayana school.

CHAPTER XII

Does It Matter What You Believe?

We've been attempting up to now to understand how one religion differs from another. Implicit in all that has been said is the assumption that religious differences are real and important.

But is this thesis valid? Does it really matter in the long run whether you're a Christian, a Jew, a Moslem, or a Buddhist?

Millions of people today, including many nominal members of Christian churches, are inclined to answer in the negative. They believe that all religions are basically the same, and that "one pathway to Truth is as good as another."

This sounds like a wonderfully broad-minded attitude, and people who hold it usually think they are being quite modern in their approach to religion.

In fact, they are simply subscribing to a very old type of religion called *syncretism*.

We encounter syncretism repeatedly in the Old Testament of the Bible. When the prophets proclaimed that there is no other God than Jehovah, they were resisting the syncretism of the Babylonian civilization that surrounded Israel. Then, as now, syncretism presented itself as an extremely tolerant and reasonable kind of faith. Babylon was perfectly willing to add Jehovah to its idol-cluttered altars, if the Jews would abandon their claim that He was the *only* god. Had the Jews not been—in the eyes of their Babylonian neighbors—narrow-minded and fanatical in rejecting these terms, the religion of Judaism would have been simply swallowed up without a trace five thousand years ago.

Christianity also encountered the temptation of syncretism in its infancy. The Roman civilization into which the Church was born was proud of its open-minded attitude toward all religions. As the historian Edward Gibbon has put it, "The various *modi* of worship which prevailed in the Roman world were all considered by the people equally useful." The Romans felt, in other words, that it didn't matter what a man believed so long as he believed *something* that would comfort him in battle and keep him reasonably honest. When Christianity first reached Rome, it was accorded a warm reception. The emperor Alexander Severus added a statue of Jesus to his private chapel, which already contained figures of numerous pagan gods.

Rome began to persecute the Christian Church only when it fought off the smothering embrace of syncretism, and stubbornly insisted that "there is no other name under heaven than Jesus Christ whereby men may be saved."

Such a claim is always anathema to syncretists, because it is a cardinal article of *their* faith that God would never condescend to reveal Himself in a particular way, at a particular time and place, and to a particular people.

Syncretism holds that there is *no* unique revelation in history, no single instance of divine self-communication that may be regarded as complete and trustworthy. Indeed, except in the sense that all of nature is a revelation of God, syncretists do not expect to find God taking the initiative in making Himself known to men. They look upon religion as an essentially human enterprise—an attempt by men to fathom mysteries that by their very nature are too deep to be comprehended in any one viewpoint. The corollary is that all religions may be partially true, but none is completely true. Thus, the syncretist believes, the only intelligent solution is to harmonize the various religious experiences and insights insofar as possible, and create one universal religion for mankind.

Syncretism has had many eloquent exponents through the centuries. They include the Roman emperor Julian, who first embraced Christianity and then turned bitterly against it when the Church refused to go along with his pet scheme for fitting Jesus into a side pocket of a "universal faith"; the French philosopher Rousseau, who held that there is a "natural religion" that men can discover simply by "listening to what God says in their hearts"; the German poet Goethe; the Austrian psychiatrist Carl Jung; and the English historian Arnold Toynbee.

In the East, syncretism has received a powerful boost during the past century from such Indian leaders as the great Hindu mystic Ramakrishna, Swami Vivekenanda, Mahatma Gandhi, and the philosopher-statesman Sir Sarvepalli Radhakrishnan. It is not surprising to find Hindu sages in this role, for, as we noted in the previous chapter, Hinduism has always been an eclectic religion. Of all the world's major faiths, Hinduism has least to lose by lumping everyone's convictions together in one vast amalgam, since it has already made room for every conceivable viewpoint, from the cool agnosticism of a Nehru to the fervid polytheism of a Nepalese villager.

Modern Syncretism

The Moslem world also has made a contribution to modern syncretism. It is the religion known as *Bahai*, which was founded in Iran during the nineteenth century by a government official named Mirza Husayn Ali. He took the title Baha'u'llah ("Glory of God") and proclaimed himself a prophet possessed of the same divine guidance as Moses, Christ, and Mohammed. Baha'u'llah offered his followers a "world faith" which, he said, harmonized and fulfilled the valid insights of all the major religions. The Bahai movement now has an international headquarters in Haifa, Israel, and claims followers in 250 countries. There are a few thousand Bahais in the United States, and some of them must be quite wealthy, to judge from the magnificence of the Bahai Temple in Wilmette, Illinois, on Chicago's north shore.

For every American who formally embraces syncretism by joining Bahai or the Vedanta Society, there are thousands of others who maintain their affiliations with Presbyterian or Methodist or Episcopal churches while espousing syncretistic views. They are attracted to syncretism for several reasons. Its open-mindedness appeals to those who remember how much suffering has been inflicted on the human race by intolerant religious zealots who were certain

that they alone possessed the true faith. Its denial that
God has revealed Himself through specific acts in history
appeals to those who think it unscientific to believe in any
kind of miracle. Its promise of a "universal" faith appeals
to those who feel a desperate sense of urgency about forg-
ing bonds of human unity in a shrinking world threatened
by atomic annihilation.

"The plausible, rationally almost self-evident character
of the syncretistic answer to the needs of the world makes
it a far more dangerous challenge to the Christian Church
than full-fledged atheism is ever likely to be," says Dr.
W. A. Visser 't Hooft, the great Dutch theologian and
ecumenical pioneer who was the first General Secretary of
the World Council of Churches.

In a splendid little book entitled *No Other Name* (The
Westminster Press, Philadelphia), Dr. Visser 't Hooft
points out that a purely materialistic view of life is not
often a serious temptation for those who are in any sense
believing Christians. Syncretism, however, *is* a temptation,
because it seems at first glance not to take anything away
from Christianity, but only "to add a wider dimension to
the faith of the Church."

That's the way it seems at first glance. But on closer
inspection, it should become obvious that Christianity
cannot come to terms with syncretism today, any more
than it could in the first century of the Christian Era. You
can have Christianity *or* syncretism, but you cannot have
both. It is necessary to make a choice between them, because they are fundamentally and forever incompatible.

The heart of the Christian faith is the assertion that
God *has* revealed Himself in history in the person of

Jesus Christ. The self-revelation that God accomplished in the Incarnation was unique, once-for-all, the crucial divine intervention in human affairs.

When Christians try to tell others the good news that "God was in Christ, reconciling the world unto Himself," they are not laying claim to any superior religious insight, Dr. Visser 't Hooft says. They are simply delivering a message that has been entrusted to them—a message that was addressed from the start to all mankind.

Why Christians Can't Compromise

Thus, Christianity professes to be precisely what the syncretist seeks—a universal faith. It does not assert that the religion of Christians is superior to the religion of Jews, Moslems, or Buddhists, but rather that Jesus Christ is "Lord of all men."

There is no way in which Christians can compromise on this assertion. Either it is the most important truth ever proclaimed—or it is a damnable falsehood which has led hundreds of millions of people astray. In neither case can it be fitted into a neat synthesis with other religions.

"We cannot participate in the search for a common denominator of all the religions," says Dr. Visser 't Hooft. "The claim which the Church makes for its Lord has its origin, not in any religious pride or cultural egocentricity, but in the message of the New Testament. For the whole New Testament speaks of the Saviour whom we have not chosen, but who has chosen us. It is possible to reject Him, but it is not seriously possible to think of Him as one of the many prophets or founders of religion."

The real tragedy of syncretism, Dr. Visser 't Hooft concludes, is that while it professes to be a bold advance beyond Christianity, "it leads in fact to a regression." For in denying that God has made a decisive self-disclosure in history, the syncretist is saying that man must rely on his own insights, speculations, and guesses for whatever clues he may have to the ultimate meaning of life.

He may put together bits and pieces of various historical religions, and call the result a "universal faith." But he can repose no more confidence in this faith than he has in the infallibility of his own judgment—for it will necessarily be his judgment that is the ultimate criterion of what is included in the synthesis, and what is left out.

Dr. Visser 't Hooft goes on to point out that syncretism is never, in practice, as all-embracing as it sounds in theory. It can include within its synthesis only those religious viewpoints that are consonant with its own fundamental denial of a definitive divine revelation. The usual formula for compounding a syncretism is to take a base of Hindu pantheism and season it with a few quotes from Moses, Christ, Buddha, and Mohammed to give it an appearance of inclusivism.

"The demand for a world faith is comprehensible," says Dr. Visser 't Hooft. "But it must not be answered in such a way that we destroy the very foundations of faith." Syncretism, with its pretensions to go beyond Christianity, is in fact a retreat into pre-Christian darkness. It confronts men with an "It," an impersonal power which they must try to figure out for themselves, rather than a "Thou," the living God who cared enough for His human creatures to take the initiative in revealing Himself to them in His Son, Jesus Christ.

If a person elects to bet his life on Christ, does it follow that he must despise and look down upon other religions? By no means. From the Apostle Paul to Pope Paul VI, leaders of the Church have taught just the opposite. The Christian has a particularly clear obligation to look with reverence and respect upon Judaism—the religion which Jesus said he came "not to destroy but to fulfill." But, as Pope Paul said on his visit to India in 1964, Christians also have "the duty of knowing better" the hundreds of millions of fellow human beings who are Moslems, Hindus, Buddhists, or followers of other faiths, "recognizing all the good they possess, not only in their history and civilization, but also in the heritage of moral and religious values which they possess and preserve."

The New Testament puts it quite succinctly: "God has not left Himself without witness at any time." In every age, in every nation and in every culture, the Christian should expect to find glimpses, and often much more than glimpses, of the Light which was focused so brilliantly in Jesus of Nazareth. But to say this is very far from saying that "all sources of Light are the same." There *is* a difference between a light bulb, even a very big light bulb, and the sun.

Other Books to Read

If you wish to delve more deeply into some of the religious faiths described in the foregoing pages, you will find a wealth of reading matter available at any good library or bookstore.

There are three books that offer particularly good treatments of the non-Christian religions, and which are easy for laymen to read and enjoy. They are *The Religions of Man*, by Huston Smith (Harper & Row); *The World's Great Religions*, by the Editors of *Life* (Time, Inc.); and *Christian Faith and Other Faiths*, by Bishop Stephen Neill (Oxford University Press). More technical and encyclopedic is *Non-Christian Religions from A to Z*, published by Grosset & Dunlap as part of its *Universal Library*.

If you want to stretch your mind, and receive a really scholarly introduction to all the significant religious viewpoints of our time, tackle *Twentieth Century Religious Thought*, by Professor John Macquarrie of Union Theological Seminary (Harper & Row, New York).

For more insight into modern atheism, you might try

Atheism in Our Time, by Ignace Lepp (The Macmillan Company); *The Varieties of Unbelief,* by Martin E. Marty (Holt, Rinehart & Winston); or *The Faith of a Heretic,* by Walter Kaufmann (Doubleday & Company).

There are shelves of books about Catholicism, of course. As a general introduction for the layman (including the Catholic layman who wants to know more about his own church), I would suggest *This Is Catholicism,* by John Walsh, S.J. (Doubleday & Company; an Image Book). Also recommended are two books written by and for Protestants: *The Riddle of Catholicism,* by Jaroslav Pelikan (Abingdon Press); and *Primer on Roman Catholicism for Protestants,* by Stanley I. Stuber (Association Press).

Judaism has also been the subject of hundreds of books. For a vividly readable account of what Orthodox Judaism means to a modern American, see *This Is My God,* by novelist Herman Wouk (Doubleday & Company). A Reform Jew's view is presented in *The Story of Judaism,* by Rabbi Bernard J. Bamberger (Union of American Hebrew Congregations). A sympathetic outsider looks at Judaism in *The Way of Israel,* by Professor James Muilenberg, a distinguished Protestant scholar (Harper & Row).

For an over-all view of Protestantism and its various theological camps, I heartily recommend *The Spirit of Protestantism,* by Dr. Robert McAfee Brown (Oxford University Press); *A Layman's Guide to Protestant Theology,* by William Hordern (The Macmillan Company); *Beyond Fundamentalism,* by Daniel B. Stevick (John Knox Press); and *The Story of the Reformation,* by William Stevenson (John Knox Press).

You'll find lively and readable accounts of the major

Protestant denominations in *The Story of America's Religions,* by Hartzell Spence (Abingdon Press) and *Churches in North America,* by Gustave Weigel, S.J. (Helicon Press). The latter is especially interesting because it was written from a Catholic viewpoint by the late Father Weigel, a great Christian who played a pioneer role in the ecumenical movement. Some of the off-beat groups not covered in this book are described in *Faiths, Cults and Sects in America,* by Richard Matheson (The Bobbs-Merrill Co.). For a more extensive treatment of Orthodoxy, you might consult *The Eastern Orthodox Church,* by Ernst Benz (Doubleday & Company; an Anchor Book).